Rug Hookers Gu

YARNIVERSE!

by Judy Taylor

Many thanks!

Featured Artists

Sigrid Grant
Ottawa, Ontario

Dianne Cross
Sydney, British
Columbia

Steve Grappe
Fulton, Texas

Karen Miller
Ottawa, Ontario

Kay LeFevre
Belle River,
Ontario

Sharon Johnston
Calgary, Alberta

Margaret Arraj
Leeds, Massachusetts

Lise Page
Mansonville,
Quebec

Heidi Wulfraat
Lakeburn, New
Brunswick

Bonnie Campbell
Ottawa, Ontario

Jackie Alcock
Corner Brook,
Newfoundland

Kathy Barlow, Kirk Henson, Hugh and Suzanne Conrod, Hooked Rug Museum of North America, Eva Leavitt, Barbara Beedy, Turner Historical Museum and Society, Natalie Pilsbury, Roxanne Tremblay, Anita O'Connor Chandler, Judy Ware Libby, Susan Carson, Sandra Fox, Dianne Maillet, Judy Dennis, Lin Schwider, Dawn Lantz, Karen Lobb, Vivian Russell Mancine, Virginia Gross, Lana Obie, Ruby Muse, Aileen Vasquez, Judy Raymond

Judy Taylor has been obsessed by rug hooking since 1992. Her first book, *Hooking With Yarn*, sold out its first printing. It was followed by *Joy of Hooking (With Yarn!)*, which won the eLit Book Awards Gold Medal, 2011. Her instructional video won the Intl' TV and Video Artists Gold Award, 1997. Her rugs can be viewed at www.littlehouserugs.com. She is currently pondering the age old question: Does this elephant make my butt look big?

Published by Little House Rugs
PO Box 2003
Auburn, WA 98071
© Copyright 2013 All rights reserved
ISBN 978-0-615-87581-1
www.littlehouserugs.com

Table of Contents

I have been hooking rugs and teaching rug hooking for over 20 years. For me, rug hooking has provided an inexhaustible font of creativity. I somehow never get bored, even though I've hooked hundreds of rugs and other projects, created custom rugs, repaired and finished many other people's rugs. I get so excited about the design that I am working on, or the many designs floating around in my head, that it is endlessly creative and fun. Beyond the creativity though, it is a true pleasure for me to hook yarn through the backing. Just hooking mind you, it doesn't really matter what I am hooking, I just love to do it.

Unfortunately, it is not that easy for a person who is interested in hooking with yarn to find information and instruction these days. There are oodles of sources if you are interested in hooking with fabric strips, from books, magazines, websites, groups, classes and retreats, but not so much for the yarn hookers. I wrote this series of books to try to fill that need, to provide instruction and hopefully inspiration for wanna-be hookers.

In my years teaching rug hooking, I have learned that it is a mistake to try to tell new students absolutely everything there is to know about this wonderful, versatile and creative craft in a beginner class. I used to get carried away with my enthusiasm, excited to talk about all the many advanced and complex styles that are possible with rug hooking, overwhelming my dear students with way more information than they needed to learn to hook.

So when I sat down to write about rug hooking, I decided to begin with the basics, everything that a new yarn hooker needs to know to get started. That book was called *Joy of Hooking (With Yarn!)*. In it the reader learned what yarns are best for rug hooking, which

backings to use, how to get your design onto the backing, learning the technique for hooking rugs with yarn, care and cleaning of hooked rugs, and a few beginner projects to start out. With the addition of over 100 yarn-hooked rugs, made by talented rug hookers from all over North America, I hoped to provide clear instruction, with a peek at what else people are doing with rug hooking, or what else is possible when hooking with yarn.

In this book, I get to go beyond the basics, to share the many styles that are possible when hooking rugs with yarn, from primitive designs to realistic portraits. We'll cover numerous dyeing techniques that make hooking complex designs easy. We'll discover what handspun yarns can do for your rug making. We'll delve into the construction and repair of old rugs.

The big difference between basic rug hooking techniques and advanced styles is the yarn. When I think

(Opposite page)
Spools 20"x26"
Designed and hooked by Kay LeFevre

4

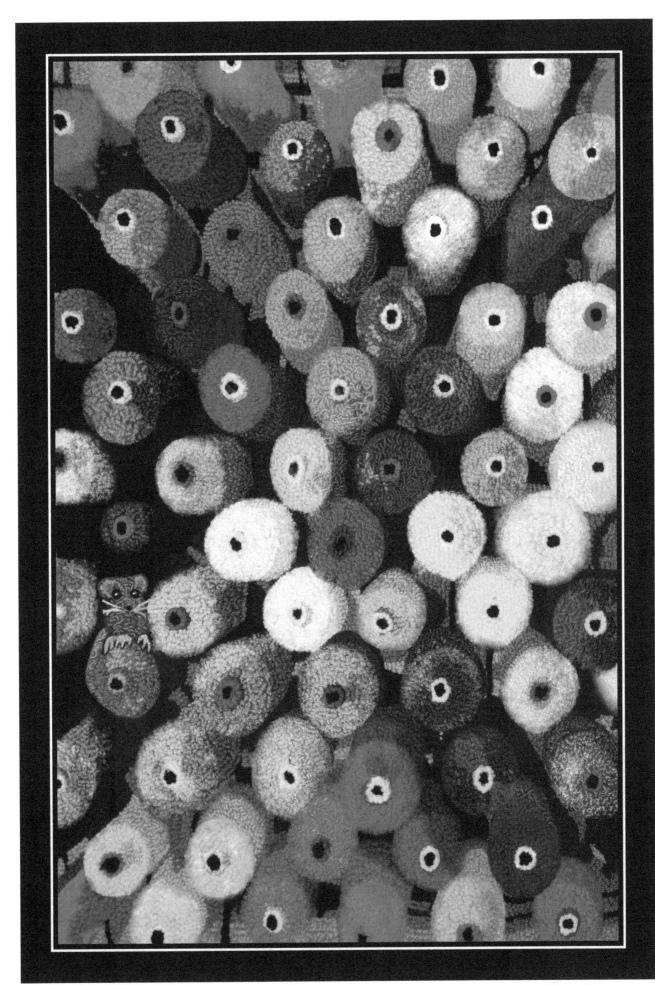

of advanced rug hooking techniques, I think of color, texture and detail. "Off-the-shelf" yarns are great, but they are not the limit of what we can create. Once you take control of the yarn, you open up a world of artistic expression to be explored.

For each rug hooker, dabbling in advanced hooking and designing techniques, there is a different way of going about things. With this in mind, I invited yarn-hooking experts to share their process, from first inspiration to finished rug. We all have our own approach, what works for one hooker may not be ideal for another, so enjoy the many perspectives offered here to inspire you in your own way.

You will find dozens of projects (starting on page 147) designed to allow you to practice the many techniques that you will find presented in this book.

Hummer 12"x16"
Designed and hooked by Kay LeFevre

COLOR

When I am color-planning a new rug design, I always begin with my stash. You know what I mean, you have one too! It's that collection of bags and boxes you've cleverly hidden in the bottom of that closet, containing all your leftover yarns from previous projects, plus the numerous impulse-buys of yarns that were such a bargain or just too pretty to pass up. The trouble with this storage system is that you don't really know what you've got, so the next rug you start, you'll be running back to the yarn store to get more yarn, instead of using the gorgeous stuff you already have!

So let's get that pretty stuff out where we can see it. My stash is displayed in milk crates, with every skein visible. That way I can tell what colors I already have, and estimate how much of each color is available. My stash consists of leftover yarns, plus yarn I've purchased, and yarn I've dyed and spun from my own flock. All the skeins are stacked, and the smaller balls of leftovers are kept in clear plastic bags, organized by color. This leftover supply is enormously useful for hit-or-miss rugs. Say you just need a little bit of red for something, you can just pull out the red bag and there you have a bunch of shades of red to choose from. If all those little balls of leftovers are tangled up in a bag, you'll never find what you need.

Having your stash organized and displayed in this way really boosts your creativity, because it is like having your own little yarn store. You will be inspired every time you look at it. I keep all my carded wool displayed in the same way, so I can see every color that I have, and about how much is there. Having all your wool and yarn on display takes up space, I know, but think about the money and time you have already invested in those lovely colors you just couldn't live without.

OK, so now you've checked out your stash, what if you need different colors for different effects? Well, then it is time to make friends with your dyepot. In this book, you will learn how to create yarns using dip-dyeing, overdyeing, progressive dyeing, blending hand-spun yarns, and using natural-colored yarns. Then you will be able to try out your new skills on a series of projects. The wonderful thing about these techniques is that none of them are difficult and all of them are versatile and interchangeble.

Small amounts of leftovers go in clear plastic bags, organized by color

MY STASH:
OK, I'll admit I tidied up a bit, but doesn't it just make you want to hook something?

Jasper 18"x24"
Designed and hooked by Lise Page

HOOKING JASPER

A friend asked me if I could hook a a rug for her her husband of a favorite Clydesdale. Now, I am not a seasoned hooker by any means, I am self-taught, and thanks to Judy's books I am learning more all the time... so of course I said "Sure, if you have a picture I could probably draw it and hook it for you."

And that is how this project began. I really wanted it to turn out as closely as possible to the real thing, seeing that she planned on giving it to her husband as a surprise gift (no pressure?).

First thing... measure and cut my linen to a size that would permit me to draw him large enough to enable some shading for his neck muscles. I serged my linen so that the end piece would give me an 18"x24" canvas to work with.

Second... put on my creative cap and sketch him out. I tend to draw directly on the linen with a black sharpie. I know there are many ways to put a design on your backing, some use grid lines and/or lighted tables, but for me direct drawing works.

Third... I went through my yarn stash and chose my colours. I have quite a variety of colours, some hand-dyed, some not, but I didn't have enough different shades of brown to do the shading. Off to the yarn stores I went, and I also found some great yarn online. I am partial to Lopi yarn and I do love Roving yarn (when hooking with Roving it gives me the look of wool strip loops and adds a little more movement).

Fourth... Once I had my yarn in hand I took a deep breath and began. I usually start on the hardest section of the rug, for this one it was the eye, then the ears and nose. I must admit hooking the bridle was a little tricky because of the stitches on the leather. When hooking with yarn and doing such small details a "one loop" detail becomes quite finicky. I hooked all my "one loops" and then hooked the halter colour around them. Sure was glad that was done! Then the neck, which was a little more challenging than I thought it would be, being a dark brown horse with a muscular neck, I had to make sure it didn't become a brown blob. So I used many different shades and textures to create waves of colour and show movement.

Fifth... hook the ribbons. Another detailed project but I got through it, phew. And the rest was a piece of cake. Following the framing I handed it over to my friend who was quite pleased, she promptly put it up on the wall to surprise her husband when he came home. Her report to me was when he came in the house he saw it right away and said "That's Jasper!" That was the best critique I could have had because he actually recognized his horse. I was thrilled!

HOOKING OLD DAYS

My husband and I just happen to love old stuff. Our house is filled with antiques we have collected over the years and they just feel like they are alive with stories of the past. I remembered seeing a picture last winter, in a magazine, of the corner of a house that had an old sleigh leaning on it, and thinking how it looked like my grandparent's old house when I was a child so long ago!

First thing... design floating around in my head.

Second... size. It was going in our bedroom between two windows so it needed to be larger than I normally make them. I purchased two yards of linen, measured it out and serged my edges.

Third... started to draw the house. I decided to include a window with a lantern burning for light, then a tree and shrub, the sleigh, a tree stump, basket of firewood for the stove. The barrel and shovel just happened.

Fourth... choosing my colours. I love blue, so the house had to be blue, and I have lots of that in my stash. Two shades of green for trees, three different yellows for the lamp and lots of browns for the sleigh, stump, logs and shovel. The snow was tricky because I had never actually hooked much of it before and what I had done was all in the same tone, no movement at all. I do have quite a few different versions of white and off-white wool yarns and also this pristine white cotton yarn so I thought I'd try them all and see what worked.

Fifth... started hooking! I always start in the most challenging area to me. It was the window and the trees. First time hooking trees, plus they had snow on them. I pulled quite a few loops out before I figured out how to make it look fairly real. I must say that was quite a frustrating section to hook.

Sixth... then I moved on to the stump, basket and wood, trying to make them look real with a little snow gathered in between the pieces; again, quite frustrating. Pulled loops out there too, my firewood looked like toothpics. So I tried using many different textures to show pieces of wood that look like they came from different types of trees. The shovel was hooked in my most bulky yarn.

Seventh... the sleigh. It's not perfect at all but it's the best I could do! Lettering was a fun first-timer also!

Eighth... the clapboard was a breeze to hook. The lopi yarn I used hooked like butter.

Ninth... the snow covered ground. I used four types of yarn on this section, different shades inserted here and there.

Finally done... took me one month to hook it, had it framed and fell in love with it! It was planned for our bedroom but since I wanted to repaint the room before I hung it, I put it up in the living room. For the life of me, I don't think it is going upstairs anymore, it just fits where it is. Oh well, I will have to think of something else for the bedroom!

Old Days 34.5"x27"
Designed and hooked by Lise Page

Surprised By Joy 35"x28"
Designed and hooked by Lise Page

HOOKING *SURPRISED BY JOY*

This rug has been my most challenging one to date. A friend of mine asked if I could hook a garden scene for her, roughly 35"x28". She wanted to frame it to hide the fireplace opening during the summer, then hang it over the fireplace in the winter. Of course, I said sure!? Now I usually hook pictorial style and my rugs end up looking like a portrait of real things (a horse, a sled, etc)... not abstract but real, so I started questioning my ability to hook this particular rug. Considering the size and the number of features I wanted to represent, I couldn't hook real roses, honeysuckles, clematis, phlox, etc... What I hooked would represent them but to me wouldn't be them!?

And so begins the planning and "doing" stages. First: I looked for inspiration on the internet, came up with a couple of ideas and sent them to her via email, but they weren't quite what she was looking for. I am a gardener by trade in the summer months and take many pictures of the gardens I work on. She happens to be a gardener also, so I pulled up some pictures of her gardens and sent them to her for approval and this is the one she chose.

Second-- As I said to her, "sure I can do this," I was thinking "me and my big mouth!?" I measured my linen, surged the edges, drew in my working frame, (marked a framed area that would contain the actual design). Drawing it on the linen was a challenge. I don't pre-draw on paper then transfer, I draw my design directly on

11

the linen, so I drew it up roughly and kept my 3"x4" colour printed copy by my side the whole time.

Third-- Choosing the colours. I have quite a stash of yarn so I went through it all, found the ones I could use and figured out what else I needed. As you can see, this rug has a tremendous amount of greens and I had quite a few but needed something special for the lawn to make it different from all the rest. Off to my favorite wool store I go, I found the perfect variegated green for my grass and purchased 2 skeins just in case I ran out and couldn't match the dye lot.

Fourth-- OK, so it's time to start hooking, where do I start? I scratched my head quite a bit on this. There are some that say hook your edges first, some say hook the center first, etc. I usually don't have rhyme or reason to my beginnings, I just start hooking. I decided to start the lawn section because I was dying to see what my new yarn would do and had a plan on how I was going to make it look like it was free moving grass. So I started with the lawn and I "wiggly-piggly" hooked it so that it swirled and moved in my eye. I do tend to hook from one end to the other of the project, which means from right to left and then left to right in about 5" sections at a time.

I ended up pulling out lots of stuff, looked back on it and didn't like it, pulled it our again, and so on... It took me a while to hook this one because I was so intimidated by all the details and because I really wanted her to like it. All those single loops that had to be pulled, before I could hook a clump of roses, phlox or ground cover, oh my how I dreaded it! The trellis was a challenge but a fun area to do. I could picture the climbing roses with the honeysuckle woven through steel supports. I actually found myself smiling through this section because I can remember the sweet scents those two flowers offer up in the early morning, when the sun begins to warm them and I'm weeding around them. Once I had hooked the actual gardens, stone walls and pool area my doubts had disappeared and I felt confident about the end results. The garden shed and trees were a breeze to hook and the end came quite quickly after that.

Phew, I was done... had shown my friend a quick picture of the rug, told her it was done but that I wasn't having it framed until I had shown my fellow-hookers at the next hook-in. I wanted them to see it because they had been my cheering section throughout the whole process; they are a great bunch of women and I thank them for their support! Couldn't help myself... right after the hook-in I went to my friend's house to show it to her... and she was thrilled (I let out a long held breath). Yeah!

I had told her that I needed to name the rug and that I wanted her to do it... "Surprised by Joy," (CS Lewis) is what came to mind and there it is! Off to have it framed this week and then into her home it goes... where it belongs.

You can view Lise's other rugs on Rug Hooking Daily (www.rughookingdaily.ning.com)

Dresden Plate Rug
19.5"x44"
Designed and
hooked by
Judy Taylor

Basic Dyeing Instructions

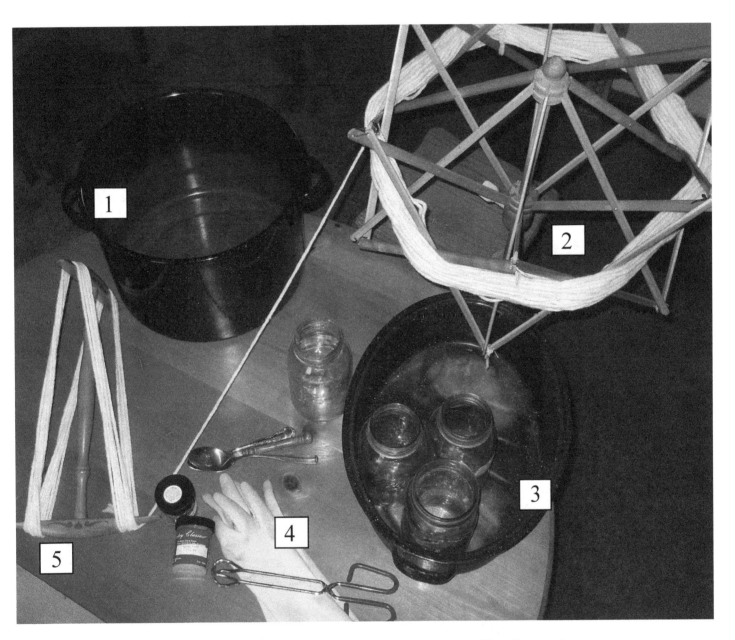

1. Large canning pot

2. Umbrella swift (optional) for holding and unwinding skeins of yarn

3. Roasting pan with mason jars

4. Dyes, spoons, rubber gloves and tongs

5. Niddy-noddy for winding yarn into skeins

BASIC INSTRUCTIONS FOR DYEING YARN A SOLID COLOR

First, let me say that I am about as unscientific as you can get when it comes to dyeing. Rather than concentrating on formulas, temperatures and timing, I tend to throw yarn in the pot and see what cool stuff comes out. In fact, most of my yarn is dyed before I know what I'm going to do with it. I get inspired by the colors and that leads me to designing something new. None of the dyeing techniques in this book are difficult, and if you don't like the results, you can overdye for something better.

If you've never dyed yarn before, here are a few basic practices for producing a solid-colored yarn. First, you will need to cross-tie your skeins so they don't get tangled in the process. I cross tie each skein three times. (Figure 6)

If you are dyeing wool yarn (or any other animal fiber like dog or silk) you will want a chemical dye that is made for dyeing animal fiber. I use Country Classics because it is really easy to use, economical and comes in a dizzying array of fun colors.

Bring water to a boil in your canning pot. You want plenty of water if you are dyeing a solid color, because you want the yarn to be able to move around freely in the water. Once your water is boiling, add the dye, but use half of what the package recommends. It is much easier to add dye than it is to take it away, so go lightly until you get the color you want.

Drop a small piece of the yarn into the dyepot, and let it soak for two or three minutes. Take it out and check out the color. Add more dye if needed. (Figure 7)

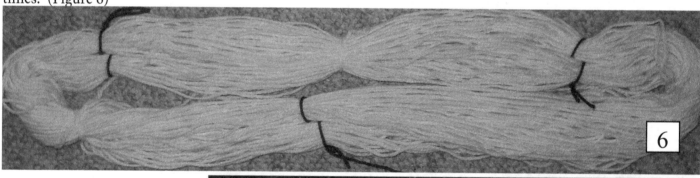

6

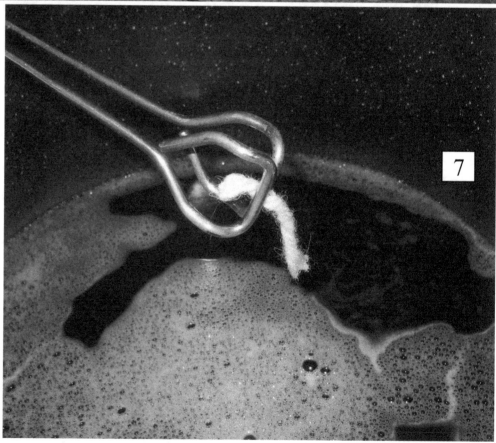

7

Lower your cross-tied skeins into the dyepot, gently pushing the yarn down so everything is in the dyebath. Let the pot simmer for about twenty minutes. When going for a solid color, it is nice if you can lift the skein up occasionally, to make sure the dye is being absorbed evenly by the wool.

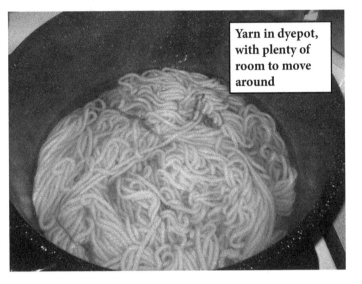

Yarn in dyepot, with plenty of room to move around

Fill another canning pot in your sink with the hottest tap water you can get. When you have filled the pot, throw in a splash of dishwashing liquid (don't put the soap in while you're filling the pot, you don't want a lot of suds). Lift the dyed yarn out of the dyepot with your tongs and lower it into the soapy pot. Pour the dye out of the first pot and fill it with very hot water. Lift the yarn out of the soapy pot, and squeeze out some of the soap. Be careful, always wear gloves, that yarn is mighty hot. Lower the yarn into the rinse pot, then empty the soapy pot and fill it again with hot water. This will be the final rinse for your yarn. If you still feel the yarn has soap residue, repeat the rinse step until the yarn is squeaky clean.

Rinsing dyed skeins

It is very important that you avoid shocking the yarn from hot to cold when it is wet. This causes the yarn to felt together into a tangled mess. Not pretty. Felting is great with wool fabric, not so nice with yarn. You can gradually cool your rinse water, so the final product is not so hot to handle, but do it slowly.

Squeeze out as much water as you can, then if you have a washing machine that lets you choose just the spin cycle, put the yarn in for a spin and it will dry much faster. If you don't have a washing machine that lets you just do the spin cycle, then you can "wuz" the wool. Go outside and grip the skein on one end, and swing the living tweedle out of the yarn. Then you can hang the yarn to dry. On a sunny day, your yarn might dry in as little as an hour. Inside in winter, you can hang your yarn, or lay it on a towel to dry.

Lift the skeins to get the dye to absorb evenly

Wuzzing the wool

These are the basic instructions for dyeing yarn a solid color. Now let's see what happens when we start to tweak the process.

One of the most fun and satisfying techniques is dyeing variegated yarns for primitive rugs. When I'm going for the rustic effect of folk designs, I want the colors to fade here and there, like they would in days of yore. Here it is important to reduce the amount of water in the dyebath, so the yarn is covered, but can't move around. Push the yarn into the dye quickly, then leave it to simmer for about 20 minutes. Don't pick it up or move it around, just leave it. Then you rinse it the same way you did the solid-colored yarn.

Resulting variegated yarns (same yarn used in the background for Brementown below)

Variegated yarn dyeing, with little room to move around in the pot

Brementown 23.5"x31"
Designed and hooked by Judy Taylor
The template to hook this rug is on p.163

16

You can add even more variation to the yarn if you sprinkle a slightly different color on top, before you have crammed the yarn down into the dyebath.

Top left: Ewenique yarn, crammed into a Turkey Red dyepot, with Blueberry sprinkled on top, then gently pushed down so the yarn is covered in the water. The yarn soaks up both colors.
Top right: Resulting two-toned yarn
Bottom: Same two-toned yarn used to hook the background for the Penny Rug

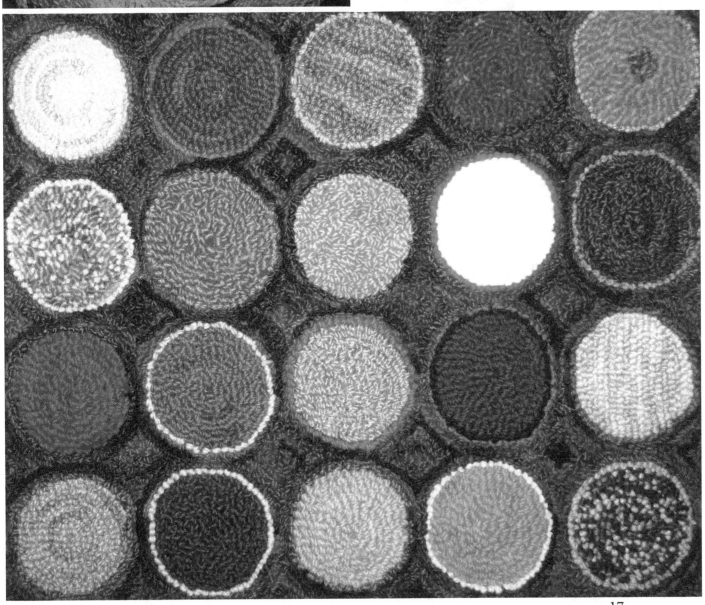

Featured Artist
Sigrid Grant
Ottawa, Ontario

This was a dyeing experiment, playing with the color wheel. I dyed all the colors specifically for the project (except the mottled purple) using Cushing Perfection Dyes and Majic Carpet pure acid dyes. Here's how I did it:

Color Wheel Star 14"x14"
Adapted and hooked by Sigrid Grant

I pre-soaked 24 small skeins in Tide (no bleach).

I mixed a small amount of dye into many different dishes with this in mind: I wanted three different values (shades) of each color in light, medium and dark, in Primary colors (yellow, blue and red) and Secondary colors (green, violet and orange) and Tertiary colors (blue-violet, red-violet, red-orange, yellow-orange, yellow-green and blue-green). For the centers, I used the light and medium shades of the Complementary colors (opposite colors on the color wheel, for example, green inside the red diamond).

I added vinegar as a mordant in each dish, and dipped each small skein into each dyebath, according to the Color Wheel.

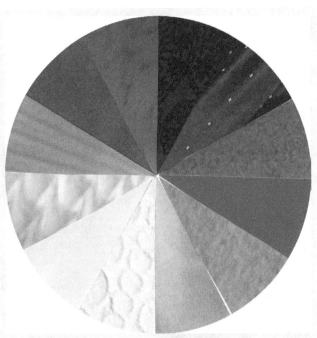

I put the dyed yarn on a cookie sheet, lined with silver foil, put a piece of foil on top and sealed it on all sides. To set the colors I steamed it in the oven, at 225 degrees for 1 1/2 hours. I rinsed the dyed yarn in warm water, squeezing gently (don't wring the yarn when it is wet). Here are the colors I ended up with (page 18).

By hooking with light and darker colors, I was able to create the 3-D effect; brighter colors make the star pattern come forward, darker colors recede for shading.

Color Wheel courtesy of Kathy Barlow at HomeWorkshop.com

Untitled 11.5"x15"
Designed and hooked by Sigrid Grant

To get the red/orange/yellow yarn for Untitled, I used one skein of yarn and dipped sections of it into red, orange and yellow dyebaths. Where the colors overlapped, they created a new color-- nice effect.

Birds of a Feather 24"x47"
Designed and hooked by Judy Taylor

Teapot Rug 29"x19"
Designed and hooked by Judy Taylor

Leftover yarns, overdyed with Pumpkin, Kiwi and Ripe Tomato dye

Overdyeing

Same yarns, hooked into Crown of Thorns, 36"x22" Designed and hooked by Judy Taylor

In *Joy of Hooking (With Yarn!)* I didn't include much on dyeing techniques, except for one project, overdyeing your leftovers. I figured that if you are reading *Joy of Hooking* it is because you want to learn to hook rugs, not a bunch of fancy dyeing techniques. Overdyeing is just so easy, and so helpful, that I thought if you only tried one dyeing project, this one will really make the most of your yarn.

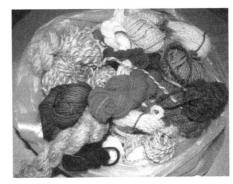

Leftovers bag, an unappealing collection of mismatched colors

May I let you in on a "trade secret?" One of the most frequent comments I get from visitors to my booth is "I love your colors!" Since I was well trained by my parents to accept a compliment, I invariably say "thank you," for the kind words and leave it at that. But I always think to myself that "color" for me is really just the result of play and happy accidents with my dyepot. It doesn't seem like I should take credit for it!

Same leftovers, overdyed with Country Classics Cornflower, Pine Green and Turkey Red, now we're talking!

When I look at a bag of leftovers (above right) I see a blah collection of yarns that don't really go together. But look what happens when I throw those odds and sods into my dyepots? Instant color, worthy of those kind words!

These overdyed yarns were used to hook Waste Not Want Not

Waste Not Want Not 31"x20"
Designed and hooked by Judy Taylor

The overdyeing project in Joy of Hooking (With Yarn!) involved taking your leftover yarns and throwing them into a couple of different dyepots willy-nilly, so that that diverse bunch of yarns are pulled together into one color scheme. You only lightly overdye the yarns, so they still retain their differences, they just come out looking like they match. Any yarn in your stash can be overdyed, so you can always transform the yarns you already have into color schemes that would make Martha Stewart proud.

To illustrate how very useful this technique can be, look at the following four rugs (Box 'O Crayons, Crown of Thorns, Cozy Rose and Haleema pp. 24-28). All of them were hooked with the same yarn. Not just the same type of yarn, the *very same yarn* was overdyed many times to create these rugs. The first one, "Box-O-Crayons" was made with the colorful array of yarns I put together for Joy of Hooking.

I wanted to illustrate the many lovely yarns that are available for hooking with yarn, in as many colors and textures that I could find. Once I had taken the pictures though, I wondered what to do with that delightful bouquet of yarn. It seemed a shame to put all of those 2 oz. skeins back into my stash, so I designed "Box-O-Crayons" to make use of this unique yarn rainbow.

Multi-colored and textured yarn array, collected for *Joy of Hooking (With Yarn!)*

Box 'O Crayons 24.5"x69.5"
Designed and hooked by Judy Taylor

Leftover yarn from Box 'O Crayons

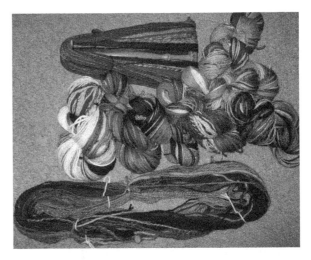

Leftover yarn from Box-O-Crayons, small bits tied end to end to create large skeins

I had lots of yarn leftover when I was done. What to do? Overdye of course! I wrapped the remaining yarn into skeins, tyeing one little ball of yarn to the last one, creating a bunch of large skeins in a variety of colors. These skeins were lightly overdyed in Very Hot Pink, Key Lime and Mountain Aqua (Country Classics). I separated the new yarns by color, and used this new color scheme to hook "Crown of Thorns."

After hooking Crown of Thorns, I still had leftovers. Back to the dyepot! This time I overdyed the leftover yarn from "Crown of Thorns" in a Mahogany dye. I separated the newly dyed yarn into dark, medium and light, and hooked the background for "Cozy Rose," using the lighter stuff in the center, and gradually going to the darker shades on the outside edge.

As you can probably guess, when I finished "Cozy Rose" I still had leftovers! Back to my trusty dyepot again! This time I overdyed the leftovers in royal blue, and ended up with the yarn I used to hook the penny background for "Haleema." So the yarn for "Haleema" was dyed at least three times, some of the original yarns were dyed to begin with, so some had been overdyed four or more times!

Again, I used the time saver of tyeing the end of one small ball of leftover yarn to the next one, while I am wrapping the yarn into skeins on my niddy noddy. That way I only had to cross-tie 7 large skeins instead of 80 little ones!

Crown of Thorns (page 24) 36"x22"
Designed and hooked by Judy Taylor

Box-O-Crayons leftovers, overdyed with Very Hot Pink, Key Lime and Mountain Aqua

These are the lefotvers after I hooked Crown of Thorns, ready for their next "makeover!"

Cozy Rose (page 25) 22.5"x32.5"
Designed and hooked by Judy Taylor

Haleema (page 26) 27.5"x34.5"
Designed and hooked by Judy Taylor

28

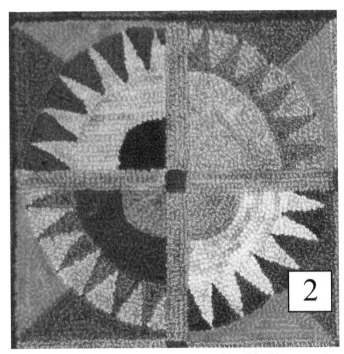

So here is the recap: I overdyed the leftovers from Box 'O Crayons (in Very Hot Pink, Key Lime and Mountain Aqua), to make the yarn I used for Crown of Thorns. I then overdyed those leftovers (in Mahogany) to make the background for Cozy Rose. And finally, I overdyed the Cozy Rose leftovers (in Royal Blue) to make the background for Haleema.

1. Box 'O Crayons

2. Crown of Thorns

3. Cozy Rose

4. Haleema

Can you believe this is all the same yarn? You can change your yarn so much, just by overdyeing!

You never need to worry about making mistakes dyeing yarn, because even if you don't like how the yarn turned out the first time, you can always overdye it. Usually, I prefer the overdyed results, because they are to totally unique.

Close up of Aurora Borealis 37"x26"
Designed and hooked by Judy Taylor

The leftover multi-colored yarns in the middle were overdyed with Slate Blue dye for the background.

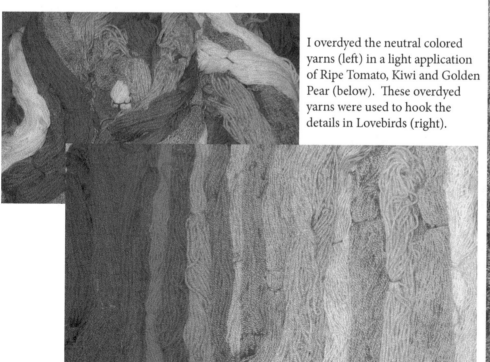

I overdyed the neutral colored yarns (left) in a light application of Ripe Tomato, Kiwi and Golden Pear (below). These overdyed yarns were used to hook the details in Lovebirds (right).

Featured Artist
Kay LeFevre
Belle River, Ontario

Bossy Cat 16"x16" Designed and hooked by Kay LeFevre

1. I opened the image or my cat, Chivas, in Photoshop. (you could use the free online program)

2. At the top menu, use Filter/Filter Gallery/Artistic/Posterize. This makes the colours stand out-- shows dramatically where each colour is.

3 I printed pages in colour (I use fast print to save ink). I used Illustrator to enlarge patterns but there's also great software called Rapid Resizer. I taped the sheets together to make a pattern.

My tip for getting the colours right is to take the eyedropper tool from Photoshop (or any colour picker) and sample several places in the design and then paint those colors on paper. I take that paper with me when I go to select my wool, which is great when I'm at the yarn store.

To me, getting the colours right is the best satisfaction (although "right" doesn't always mean perfect to the photo. If I use the exact color and hate it, I just use the one that pleases me).

4. I used Sulky transfer pens to make my pattern. I drew over the printed design with a Sulky transfer pen (use different colours if you want to remember which colour to use when hooking). Remember any text will have to be flipped or it will be backwards!

I ironed the Sulky pattern to the backing. (I use cotton rug warp. I like how it grabs and keeps the yarn.) I taped the pattern to the backing so it wouldn't move. Be careful not to push the iron around, lift and press each area. You will see the ink get darker where it has adhered to the backing.

Amazingly, you can re-use this transfer material several times!

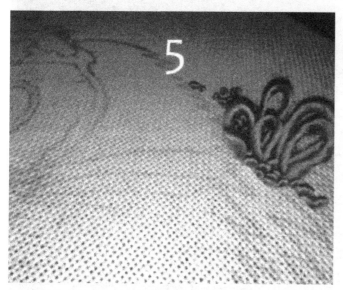

5 & 6. When I hooked the fur, I made short loops spaced out with gaps, and then make larger loops in the gaps, to be cut later. To make the fur look real I hooked progressively larger loops down the cat's body, and then cut the loops in half on top.

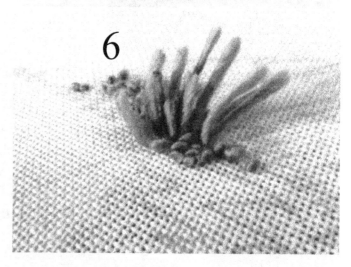

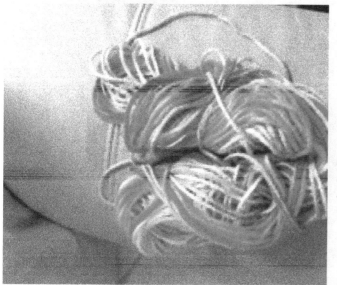

The background is so simple you will laugh. It's just a skein of "I Love This Yarn" in colour "Tangello Stripe." As each colour appeared, I stayed in a circle or group to make it appear like a shape. Then when the colour changed I moved on to the next area. This is a great trick with any variegated yarn.

You can view more of Kay's work on her Facebook page: The Wool Genie

Dip-dyeing

Close up of Serendipity, showing dip-dyed yarn
for shading (complete rug is shown on page 1)

DIP-DYEING YARN

If your design calls for realistic shading, try dip-dyeing. This easy method allows you to create shading just by hooking the yarn in the direction that you want. Say you are hooking a rose; you start hooking the darker end of the dip-dyed yarn in the inside of the petal, and simply hook toward the outside of the petal. The yarn does the shading for you, and makes you look like a rug hooking genius.

To create a dip-dyed yarn, you begin by wrapping small skeins around a paperback book or box. Wrap the yarn 40 times, and tie a piece of contrasting yarn on the top and bottom of the skein (figure 1). Then slip the skein off the box and do a figure eight cross-tie through the middle (figure 2). You can use the contrast yarn on the top and bottom to tie two or three skeins together into a bundle (figure 3).

Now fill your mason jars with about one inch of water each, and add water to your roasting pan so the jars are sitting in about one inch of water. Bring the water to a boil, and add the dye. You are going to add a tiny amount in each jar to begin with (figure 4). Drop a sample piece of yarn into each jar, and let them sit for about two minutes. You are trying for something like the darkest color of your shading. Check the samples and add dye if necessary. Again, go slow, you can add dye later in the process too, so if your samples are a bit lighter than the intended color, you can darken them later. It is nearly impossible to take color away, if you've added too much, so start light, and add color as needed.

Rinse the bundles according to the directions on page 15. If some skeins have been taken out and allowed to cool, then rinse them with water that is about the same temperature. To give you an idea of how much yarn to

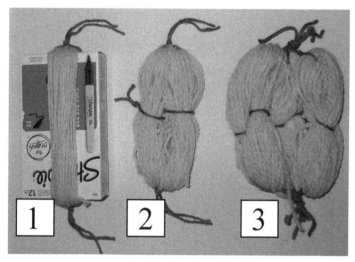

Wet one of the bundles in the boiling water in the roasting pan, then lower the bundle into one of the mason jars, letting just the first half inch sit in the dye to begin with (figure 5). You can use a spoon to keep the bundles up at the beginning. Then begin to slowly let the yarn go lower in the dyebath, gradually allowing more yarn to absorb the dye (figures 6-8). You want to avoid sudden changes of color. You can check the bundles by taking them out of the jar and letting them lay down in the roasting pan. If you are happy with the gradation of color, but want more, you can now add a smidge more of the dye to the jar, and dip the bundle again to soak up a bit more color. It is nice to have one bundle on the lighter side, and another a bit darker, then you have even more ability to create shading and contrast.

Figure 5: Use a spoon to hold up the bundle, so that just 1/2 inch of the yarn is sitting in the dye

Figure 6: Remove the spoon and let the bundle sink down a little more into the dyebath

Figure 7: Push the bundle down further, gradually letting more and more color into the yarn

Figure 8: Push the bundle all the way down into the dyebath. Notice how most of the dye is exhausted at this point. What little was there is totally soaked into the yarn.

dip-dye, I like to have two bundles on hand to hook a rose about 3" in diameter.

When the bundles are dry, cut them top and bottom, so each skein produces 80 dip-dyed pieces of yarn. You can simply tie the bundles together, or roll them up in a fabric holder, so all your dip-dyed yarns can be seen at once while you're hooking, and they won't get lost in your rug hooking bag. The fabric holder is simply one narrow piece of fabric, around 12"x24" and another piece about 4"x36". Pin the narrow fabric down, lay a bundle of dip-dyed yarn, lay the narrow piece over the bundle and pin, and repeat this for each bundle.

Figure 9: When the bundles are rinsed and dry, cut them on each end, so you have 80 6" strands

This picture shows the bundles being lowered into the mason jars. Notice that I use the roasting pan, so I can see the jars. The roasting pan has only about 1" of water in it, and each jar also has 1" of dyebath. The spoons help to keep the bundles from sinking too fast.

35

Figure 10: When you are working with dip dyed yarn, it is helpful to use a fabric holder. This can be made with a piece of fabric 8"x24" and a piece that is 3"x36." Pin the narrow fabric down on the wider piece, lay down one bundle of cut yarn, pin the narrow fabric snugly around the bundle, then lay down another bundle, pin, and so on. This fabric holder can be rolled up so you don't lose bits of yarn in your rug hooking bag (right).

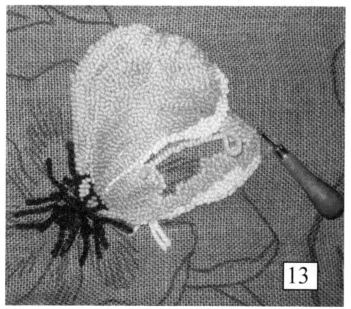

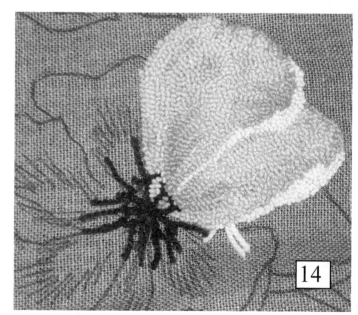

Hooking the magnolia in Serendipity (shown in close up on page 33):

I first dyed the light pink yarn for my base color (the white on the edges of the petals is the original color). Then I made the small skeins for dip-dyeing with the pink yarn. I hooked the inside of the petal first, starting with the dark end of the strand, and hooking outwards toward the paler end. (This means you have lots of ends.) I did the same thing on the outside edges of the petal, starting with the dark end on the outer edge of the petal, and hooking toward the center (figure 11). Then I hooked around all those ends with my pink base color, so I could cut them off (figure 12). I hooked the remaining petal with the pink base color, hooking in rows so that any variation in the dye would look like shading going up and down each petal (figure 13). Figure 14 shows the finished petal.

Left, pink base color. Right, same yarn dip-dyed

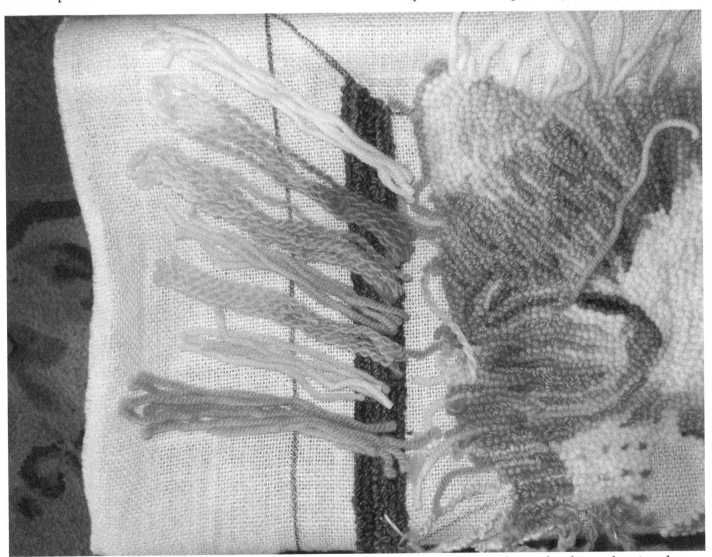

I used a whole series of gold and light brown dip-dyed yarns to hook Lady Teasle, randomly overlapping the colors.

Lady Teasle 20"x19"
Designed and hooked by Judy Taylor

You will find several practice
projects like this Rose mat
(right), to practice your dip-
dyeing, starting on page 154.

Lenore 15.5"x19"
Designed and hooked by Judy Taylor

Progressive Dyeing

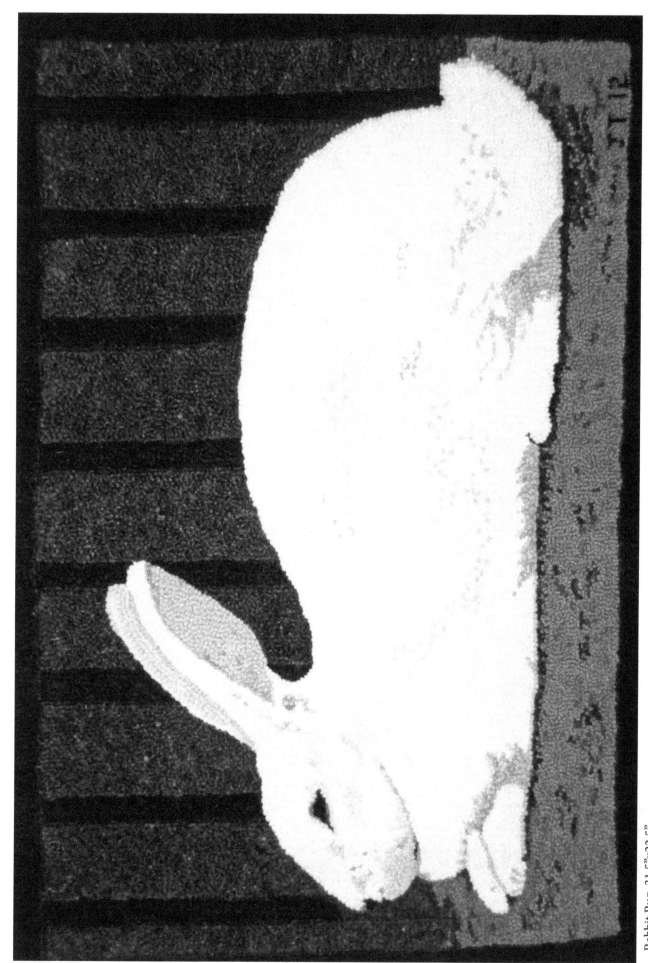

Rabbit Rug 31.5"x22.5"
Designed and hooked by Judy Taylor

Dip-dyed yarns are great for shading that is regularly repeated, like the petals of a flower, but if you are shading a large, irregular area, like in a portrait, I like to do progressive dyeing. Put three skeins of the yarn into a very light dyebath (the lightest color of shading that you are going for) (Figure 1). Let them simmer for fifteen minutes, then remove the skeins, add a smidge more dye to the dyebath and return two of the skeins to the pot (Figure 2). Let them simmer for fifteen minutes, then take them out and add another smidge of dye. Return one of these skeins back into the dyepot, and let simmer for 15 minutes (Figure 3). With this method, you can hook with one shaded color to another, as needed.

The original color, plus three shades of grey

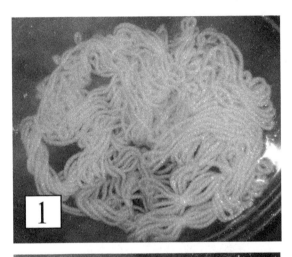

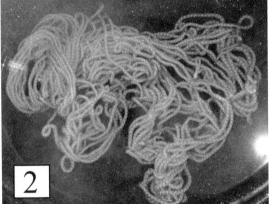

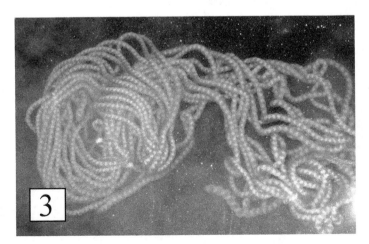

41

Another twist on the progressive method is to overdye three slightly different skeins of yarn, very light, light and medium in color, and put them into a fairly weak dyebath. You want just enough dye to make the lightest shading color for your project. Your dip-dyed and progressively dyed yarns work great for this method, but you can also get interesting results from off-the-shelf yarns. This is a great way to provide both color gradation and texture differences, which can be very helpful to make the shaded areas clear.

I overdyed these neutral colors in a pale blue dye to hook the baby's jacket

I overdyed these lighter colors in a dark blue dyebath to hook the jeans

The Great Easter Egg Hunt in progress

42

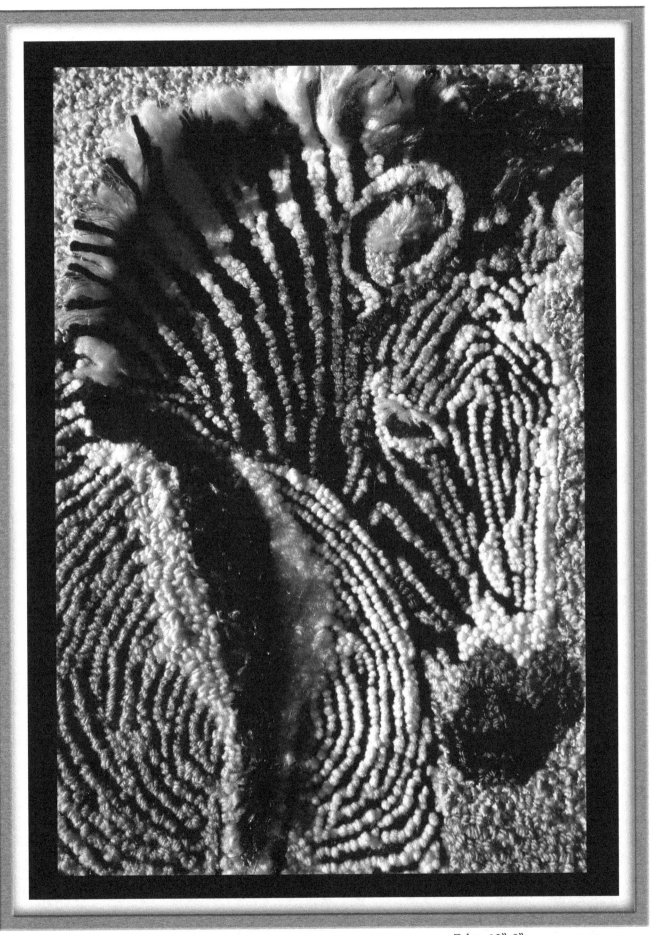

Zebra 13"x9"
Designed and hooked by Kay LeFevre

43

Featured Artist
Heidi Wulfraat
Lakeburn, New Brunswick

Love on the Run 27"x53"
Designed and hooked by Heidi Wulfraat

Love on the Run was the first rug that I hooked. While visiting the state of New Hampshire I had become enchanted with rug hooking as a form of story telling and decided that I would like to give it a try.

Animals have always been central to my life, so my dog Farmer seemed a natural choice for a rug design. At the time of hooking this rug, I had neither rug hooking classes under my belt, nor any particular exposure to the technical aspects of rug hooking. The unintentional result was that I allowed myself to focus only on Farmer, her joyfulness and companionship. What I learned was that producing a piece of work that is personal and heartfelt will always outweigh "the rules." If you're worried about your rug hooking technique, set your reservations aside, put a piece of yourself on the canvas and all else will become peripheral.

Does this mean sloppy work is OK? Not at all. I believe that when you are creating an image that is truly unique, in your own voice, and in your own style, you will be so connected to and respectful of your subject matter that you will want to present it with the best possible technique. Good craftsmanship will come with your level of interest.

Designing *Love on the Run* involved my being surrounded with photos of Farmer. I drew her figure directly onto the canvas using a heavy marker. If you find drawing free-hand a little daunting, there are several methods of transferring an outline from a photo to canvas. I would urge you to use photos that you have taken yourself so that, again, you will have a personal connection. Be fearless in marking your canvas. You have nothing to lose! Your marks will disappear as you hook.

I usually draw my pattern using a green sharpie marker, make corrections with a red sharpie and make my final decisions using a black marker. There is lots of leeway for rethinking things and making changes throughout the entire process.

I am a handspinner at heart. It is natural for me to reach for yarn when hooking. In fact, I hook with yarns of all weights and textures and with unspun fibres as well. I use premium linen backing which will accommodate tight packing of very fine yarns and will open nicely for my bulky handspun singles. I choose my materials according to colour, and when the colour that I'm hoping for is not within reach, I head to the dyepots!

Angus 62"x42"
Designed and hooked by Heidi Wulfraat

44

I am currently hooking in an abstracted format, again from a very personal perspective. This series of fractured images embrace my less-than-stellar eyesight, and speaks of an alternative way of seeing things. *My* way of seeing things! Along the way I decided that this work should be hooked in handspun yarn. I came to realize that by spinning and dyeing for these rugs, the conception of each image became very clear to me. After this additional time spent in thought and preparation I found the hooking itself to be very straightforward and well-planned. Alternatively, one might spend additional preparation time working in a sketchbook, in collage, or on a photo expedition.

For me, personal connection is the key. Hook a subject matter that is near to your heart, express a personal belief, or a personal commentary. Use materials that are meaningful to you; yarn that you have recovered from your child's first sweater, flannel taken from your husband's favorite work shirt that has finally been retired, handspun yarn that you have made yourself or that has been gifted to you by a dear friend. These are the ingredients that will set you free to hook in your own style with exciting and satisfying results.

Aside from a country fibre shop, I manage a small flock of sheep. Our farm has a no-kill, no-sell policy, so these girls have been around for a good period of time, providing me with fleece all the while. I am connected to these animals. I know all of their names. I am deeply connected to the fleece that I wash and card, the yarn that I spin and then hook. Connection is a powerful thing. It allows you to forge ahead with less hesitation. It just feels right. What are your connections? Your stories are unique. They will empower you and inform your work. Be yourself and hook with abandon.

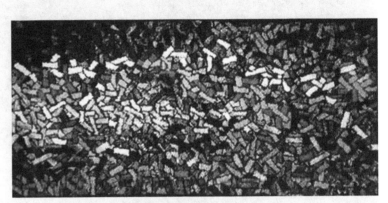

Wildflowers 42"x25"
Designed and hooked by Heidi Wulfraat

Tribute To Tiffany 29"x24"
Designed and hooked by Heidi Wulfraat

My Little Petunia 24"x24"
Designed and hooked by Heidi Wulfraat

Handspun Yarns

One of the best ways to get interesting colors and textures for rug hooking using handspun yarns. One of the great features of handspinning is that we can blend colors for a heathered effect, which is difficult to achieve if you dye yarns. Don't worry, I'm not going to insist that you learn to spin yarn, you can find hand spinners in your area by searching for spinning guilds on the internet. There is likely a spinning group that meets in your very own town and welcomes visitors. There you can find a handspinner that can create the perfect yarn for your project.

I blended four colors of wool, (light brown, beige, white and pink/orange) to create different skin tones and shadows for The Great Easter Egg Hunt (shown in progress below).

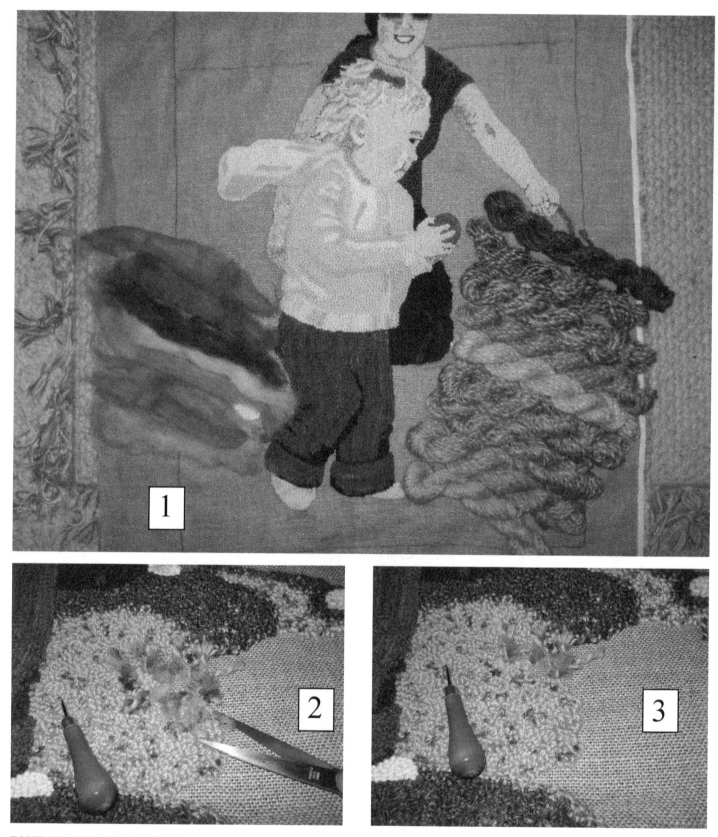

PLYING COLORS IN HANDSPUN YARN

Plying different colors together allowed me subtle color changes in the grassy area of The Great Easter Egg Hunt.

My base color for the grass was the light green roving on the bottom left of the above photo (figure 1). I spun a single ply (strand) of each of the other wool colors, and plied it with the pale green base color.

On the top right of the photo (figure 1) is a dark brown/green variegated wool. I spun up a two ply yarn of this as well, so I could use it for the shadow.

By periodically hooking bits of each yarn, I was able to create the effect of detail in the foreground, fading off toward the distance. Figure 2 shows the tails of many different colors, figure 3 shows what the grass looked like after I was able to trim off the tails.

I used the same technique of blending color and plying colors for the grassy area in the Jacob Farm Rug.

Jacob Farm Rug 36"x25"
Designed and hooked by Judy Taylor

I used a combination of handspun and commercially spun yarns to make the Charlie Mat.

Charlie Mat 12"x17"
Designed and hooked by Judy Taylor

49

Chimp on her Shoulder   16"x20"
Designed and hooked by Kay LeFevre

(opposite page)
The Great Easter Egg Hunt 23"x32"
Designed and hooked by Judy Taylor

Burzies Cottage 20"x20"
Designed and hooked by Dianne Cross

All of my imagery begins with an emotional commitment in me. Both these buildings are owned by dear family members in Britain. And having stayed in each of them as a guest, I wanted to return my thanks in the form of a rug hooking.

I took photographs in order to be able to work from an image when I returned home. The photos were then enlarged in gray scale to the size that I wanted. After selecting only the details I felt needed, I transferred the image I wanted using an indelible pen onto the red dot fabric. It is important that one does not attempt to replicate all photographic details, that only the key elements are transferred. Once done, the image was again transferred onto a backing. I choose linen over burlap as I feel it is more durable.

The purpose of the imagery in these rugs was to create an interpretation of these lovely homes. In order to achieve this, the handling of colour and texture is critical and cannot be achieved in the same way with commercial yarns. Our eyes are used to seeing not solid fulsome colour in most of our world but colours muted,

Maison de Compagne 20"x20"
Designed and hooked by Dianne Cross

MAISON DE COMPAGNE

blended, mottled with shades of the same colour and even intermixed with different colours. We interpret our world through its imperfections. I needed to achieve this sense of imperfection in order to reach the natural feeling I wanted them to possess. I could not achieve this with commercial yarns.

I next do a colour analysis to determine the palette for the piece. Beginning with a selection of pre-dyed rovings and then using either hand cards or a drum carder I begin blending shades of like colours in different percentages. For instance, in starting on the building in Burzes Cottage, I chose rovings in several brick shades, and included a little gray. I carded in recorded percentages, then spun a sample. When satisfied, I carded and spun a variety of yarns in various shade combinations to create the imperfections of the natural world. In *Maison de Compagne,* I worked with a gray palette, carding various shades, including white. Each of the coloured areas are treated in the same way.

The resulting yarns are not only able to create the colour and shades desired, but also the thickness and textures can be modified. While I do use two-ply in some cases, I find cable yarns very useful. Cables lend themselves to additional mixing of colour. Another reason I feel that cables are valuable is that they sit nicely once hooked in the fabric. An easy way to make a cable yarn is to break off about a yard of two-ply yarn, tie it to a spindle and overtwist it, then fold back to produce an 18" cable yarn. This can be done, of course, on a spinning wheel in greater lengths (more about cabling your own yarns later).

I use a variety of hooks while working in order to lessen any stress on my arm and wrist. I usually begin with my work in a hoop as it is easy and convenient. As the piece progresses, I transfer it to a square gripper hook frame. You must be careful though with using gripper hooks and yarn. It is easy to pull your work out as you remove your piece, so be careful to remove it gently!

I watch my directions in hooking. In these two architectural pieces I hooked the sky and lawn in horizontal straight lines while using a swirl pattern in the vegetation. Each building had surface details which I simplified in the hooking, putting in enough of them to allow the eye to complete the surface texture. In Burzes Cottage, small areas of darker colour were used to create an impression of the colour ranges of the bricks on the building. In the Normandy farmhouse, the use of darker wool served the same suggestive purpose on the stone building.

Hooking these pieces depends on the interaction of the viewer with the work. They require the viewer to recognize the natural image that is being suggested to them. For those who are connected to the homes, I hope their emotional attachment is aroused, and for those who are just viewing, I hope that they will sense the peace and beauty built into these homes.

My desire to hook birds coms from my emotional attraction to them. Starting with the design image. I work from photos, but the final image may be a blend of several photos for both prime components and backgrounds. I copy photos in grayscale (grayscale helps in developing value and shades in the final colours of yarns you select), combining parts needed in collage style on a background sheet. Enlarge as desired; if you need something larger than 11"x17", then take the final photo copy to a commercial printer for enlargement.

I select burlap for any piece that I know will not last too long, for example, mug rugs, hot mats, etc. I use linen for any piece that I feel is significant and should be long-lasting.

I use cotton warp also, it is durable and very easy to work with, ideal for a piece which will be worked on while travelling as it does not shed like burlap. I use monk's cloth when I want flexibility in the finished piece (like pillows or tea cozies) because it is softer than any of the other backings.

I have a significant stash of rovings and commercial yarns in a wide range of colours. I store all yarns in see-through, shallow Rubbermaid under-bed containers, organized by colour. The main choice for me will always be wool from a sheep with a wool count upward from 25 microns for durability; any count lower than 25 microns (such as Merino) is suitable for small pieces where durability is not an issue. For lustre and increasing durability, I like to blend some mohair (40% mohair/60% wool). For special effects I frequently card wool with dog hair and I sometimes use silk plied with wool yarn.

For a range of colours, I will card together different shades of rovings in various percentages to achieve the effect I want. I vary the carding for final effect; sometimes I card the colours thoroughly for an even shade. At other times, when I want spots of colour, the blending can be minimal so that the individual colors will show up in the spun yarn.

Handspun yarns give the options of thickness; thick single plies or medium-thick two-plies, or among my favorites, cable yarn using four single plies. I find cable yarns "snug" into the backing spaces in a secure way. An additional benefit of the cables is the greater range of colour effects the four-ply cables can provide. Cabling yarns is possible to do even if you don't have a spinning wheel. (See instructions for cabling yarns on page 184)

I scour thrift/charity shops for left-over yarns from tapestry kits to build my stash. Usually such kits use 100% wool. Often these commercial yarns are quite thin, so cabling is essential to thicken the wool to be used in the hooking. The cabling also gives me the opportunity to create a palette of colour blends and shading.

Junco 15"x15"
Designed and hooked by
Dianne Cross

Napping in the Nip 16"x20"
Designed and hooked by
Dianne Cross

Run Rabbit (in progress) 16"x16"
Designed and hooked by Dianne Cross
The background yarn is cabled, 40% mohair,
60% wool.

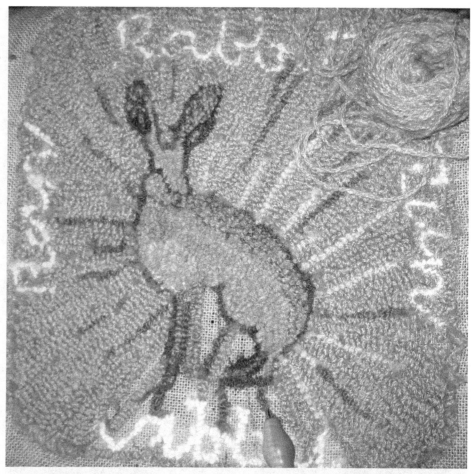

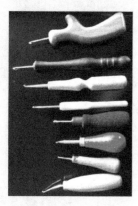

Hooks (from top to bottom)
ergonomic hook, pencil hook, pencil
hook with tapered shank, soft grip,
soft grip, old hook (approx. 50 years
old), generic hook, old hook

When I first learned to hook, I always left the outline for the border area to the last, but I now find it much easier to do the outline first. Once the border is in place, I work with a hoop at least 12" in diameter. Smaller frames are usually too light and flimsy to be effective. Because I next work on with the central portion of the image, a hoop at this stage is very easy to use and transportable (great for traveling!). If I am working in my studio, I will move to a frame to finish the larger surrounding parts of the image.

I like to have a range of different hook styles and handle shapes which helps my hand and wrist. One of my favourites for hooking with roving is a pencil hook with a substantial taper to the hook's shank. It enlarges the space in the backing for the delicate roving to pass through.

It is worth noting, particularly in working in large areas, a change in hooking direction will be discernible and will modify the colour due to the difference in the way the light hits the yarn. On the other hand, sometimes I deliberately make this change to produce an effect that I want.

Homeward 16"x20"
Designed and hooked by Dianne Cross

Using red dot fabric to transfer the design from the enlarged photo to the backing

Pascal 20"x12"
Designed and hooked by Dianne Cross

Pascal was visiting when he was one year old, and he was so inquisitive, active in discovering the world and would look out of the french doors to see all he could. I thought a back view would best convey his curiosity. I angled the perspecive to give depth and proportion. I hooked various parts by following the angled planes and vertical planes as appropriate. I hooked the garden beyond the window in various directions using a variety of hand-dyed cabled yarns. I hooked the coveralls vertically, except for the creases (which were hooked first).

You can view Dianne's other rugs at www.members.shaw.ca/spincros.

Primitive Rug Hooking

Mort & Woody 60" round
Designed and hooked by Judy Taylor

PRIMITIVE RUGS

The appeal for me of primitive rug hooking is the freedom of color and design that it allows. Lines can be crooked, details oddly shaped, features out of proportion. Pretty much anything goes with primitive rugs. Colors can also be unusual and surprising. You can doodle to your heart's content with a primitive project. No other type of rug project is more personal, more individual, more original. Whenever I see a primitive rug, I think about the person who hooked it.

Lovebirds 21.5"x30"
Designed and hooked by Judy Taylor
(You will find the design to make this rug starting on page 157)

Counting Sheep 17.5"x40"
Designed and hooked by Judy Taylor

59

The basic theme of primitive rug hooking for me is that I'm trying to make a new rug appear old and weathered. Variegated and overdyed yarns in muted colors work best.

This Welcome Home rug features both variegated and overdyed yarns. The colors red, orange, yellow and green were overdyed from various neutral-colored yarns (see photo on page 30). The background was unevenly dyed chestnut.

When hooking with the overdyed yarns, the varigation comes from the different shades and textures of the various yarns, so I used plenty of water in the dye-bath to overdye the yellow, red, orange and green.

The brown background yarn was dyed in the primitive fashion, so I wanted uneven color, fading from dark to light. This means I needed less water in the dyepot, so that when I pushed the yarn into the dyebath, there was no room for it to move around, there was just enough liquid to wet the yarn. That way, some parts of the yarn take up a lot of dye, other parts take on less.

This variegation is crucial when going for old, weathered looking designs. You can hook around the design elements in rows, echoing the details.

Welcome Home 32"x17"
Designed and hooked by
Judy Taylor

60

I used the same technique for the background yarn for the Shakespeare Sheep rug. I packed the Ewenique yarn into a strong Slate Blue dyebath. By hooking in a swirling pattern, I emphasized the variegation.

Shakespeare Sheep Rug 35"x24"
Designed and hooked by Judy Taylor

61

When drawing a primitive pattern, I find it helpful to use my non-dominant hand. I try for rough shapes, including the outline of the rug, and using my non-dominant hand, these features naturally come out oddly shaped. If I draw with my dominant hand, I tend to get critical, but if I go with the left hand, I can let the features just happen. I don't do much erasing of my pencil drawing. I try to keep the first impression whenever possible.

If you have the right yarn for the project, primitive rug hooking is so easy. I love hooking primitives because they are fast projects. I tend to use bulkier yarns, and the designs are simple and easy to follow.

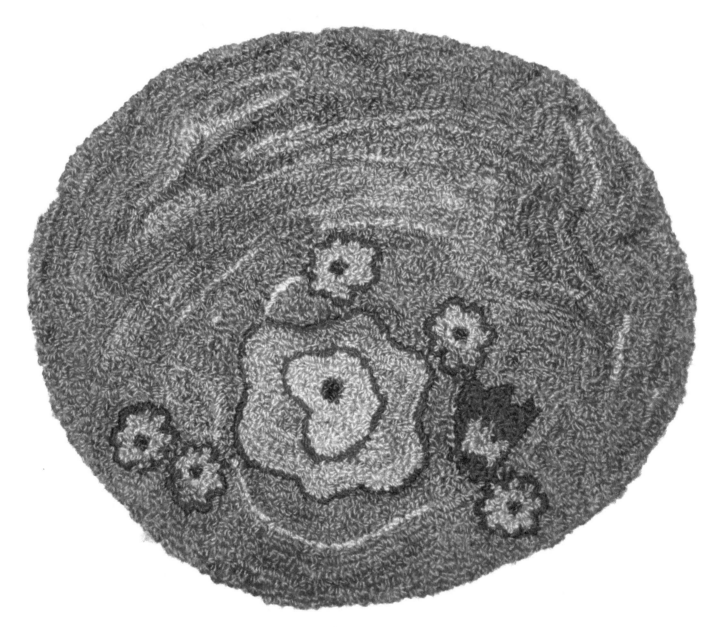

Primitive Bunny Mat 14"x18"
Designed and hooked by Judy Taylor

Another fun technique for creating primitive yarns is to dye with more than one color. In the Primitive Bunny Mat, I dyed Ewenique yarn using bluberry dye, with turkey red sprinkled on top. This yarn changed color as I hooked, so without any effort, the background echos the details.

Featured Artist
Jackie Alcock
Corner Brook, NL

Eight Sisters 22"x43"
Designed and hooked by Jackie Alcock

I just started a new line of painting featuring the female form. I knew the design would lend itself well to the rug world. I drew seven female forms on a piece of burlap, one for each of my sisters and started from there. Newfoundland, where I live, is often more on the cold side, therefore all my figures are wearing coats. Now that unplanned part; I was listening to the radio when Dolly Parton's voice drifted in singing *Coat of Many Colors*. My mind drifted back to my childhood. I was the second youngest and when I was growing up I didn't get to see much new clothes, therefore I decided that whatever ends of wool that were in the end box I would use to make the coats. The sisters were centered in the middle of the rug, with a lot of space for the sky and ground. I am told I often overdo things, I pulled out the sky four times before I admitted to myself that a plain light blue sky was all that was needed for this piece.

Bling detail in *Eight Sisters*

My husband would look over to my wool corner of the TV room and see the ever-expanding rug. I explained to him what I was up to. I was hooking a rug of all my sisters. He looked at me and said, so you're doing the Witches of Westmount (his nickname for the sisters ever since the crystal ball incident at the Edmonton, Toronto and Halifax airports... another story... I digress). My mind thought, almost all my sisters own cats, I had not started the ground area, why not give each sister a cat? I added the cats.

In the meantime I went to rug camp (this rug took about seven months to complete) where I did a course on wool dyeing. I made my light blue for the sky. I noted that maybe there was also too much sky, therefore I added in trees, which was ok because I also dyed greens and browns at camp. I had all the colours covered, or so I thought. I ended up about 18 square inches short on my fern green, a common colour, which was out of stock almost right across the island. Everywhere I traveled on the island I looked for the fern green. While in St. Anthony, I, like any rug hooker, went on the Grenfell tour, where I found my fern green in the Grenfell Shop. I almost got down on my hands and knees in thanks.

My mind never stops and that is why the rug, *The Eight Sisters,* only has seven sisters in it. Like the mother who is never in the photo (because she is the one taking the photo), I am hooking the rug, therefore I am not in the rug, but my cat is. Guess which one! Oh, when I finally finished the rug there was still something missing, so I added some "bling," by giving each sister a pair of earrings. After all, what is a woman or witch without a little sparkle?

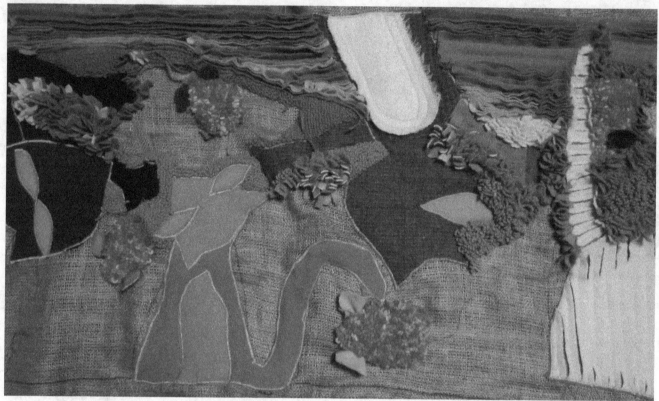

Close up of Cats & Psychedelic Mice at Dusk in progress

When I do a project it can take years for things to come together. *Cats & Phychedelic Mice at Dusk* is one such project.

First, a word of advice; you should not go to the local library discarded book sale. It is when you are rumershing through the thousands of books in that last pile on the very bottom you spy the word *rug*. Being just a beginner means that you have very little in your home stack of books that deals with rug hooking. So you do what comes naturally, when the word *rug* is recognized it hits the "crow nerve center" of your brain so you dive for the kill. You start removing books to get down to the bottom, while trying not to draw attention to yourself and that jewel on the bottom of the stack. Your hands reach the book, and you bring it up to the surface of the pile. The cover hits the light of day and you know your hunt has been worth it. You look down and see in your hands a 1971 book, "Handmade Rugs From Practically Anything" by Jean Ray Laury and Joyce Aiken. You skim through it, mind receives the message, 18 chapters and 18 ways to make a rug. You quietly walk towards the cash register, pay the lady and rush home with your jewel of a find. For a day or two you study the book. What it offers is far from what you can do at this time. You add the book to your shelves of art books, and it disappears into the landscape of your art room.

Cats & Psychedelic Mice at Dusk 8'x20"
Designed and hooked by Jackie Alcock

Then a mere year or two later, maybe three, your daughter moves into an older house and she and her boyfriend are looking for a 22"x8' rug for their upstairs hallway. Now that bug has been set in my brain-- daughter needs rug, I am a hooker, I could make a rug out of all the stuff I have been hoarding for the last five years. Could I do it for Christmas just two months away? No problem!

Now if I could do things simply I would be a well-known artist, but my creative juices kick in and the simple becomes not so simple. I remembered the book. Yes, *that rug book*. By using some of the techniques from the book, I could cut the hooking time down by doing the cats as machine appliques. This was daunting. Grade 7 Home Ec. Sewing Class didn't prepare me for this.

I dusted off my sewing machine. It made this whiney sound, like something about to die a slow and painful death. My hubby, bless his heart, took the thing apart and did his magic,  and the machine is now sounding pretty good, at least the tortured whine has been silenced.

I cut up an old blue wool blanket to use as the first layer, and I used old coats to make the top layers of the cats. I would sew these cats onto the burlap to save me half the hooking. Well, the primitive burlap tended to stretch, pull and bunch up as I sewed the cats on. It took almost a day for each cat. I sewed the edges of the cats to the burlap more than once. I am not a quick learner.

I was asleep and in a dream I saw my applique cats chasing colorful mice. In my dream, it was dusk and it was dark on one side, not so dark on the other and there was a beam of light down the middle. I woke up thinking Cat and Psychedelic Mice at Dusk. This would be what I would work towards.

I realized that this now heavy appliqued rug was not going to fit into any hoop or on any frame, but because it was so heavy, I was able to work on the rug just laying it on my TV room end table. I cut the strips up and began pulling them through. There was a problem though, the cut strips covered a lot of the cats.

65

I did what I always do when I have a problem. I went to bed and put the question to my brain. "I am hooking a rug and I cannot use a hoop or frame, the strips cover too much, what should I do?" With no distractions, working through many scenarios my brain gave me a workable solution. I used my needle punch to fill in around the cats and give the mice their nice high texture. I love to do scupltured rugs and discovered a few years ago that a needle punch worked wonders for this technique. I needle punched as usual but held onto the hooked end as I pulled the needle back. This gave me more height and in this case, much fuller hooking.

My cat was my constant companion while I was working on the rug, sitting on one end or attached to the ball of wool I was using. At times I found a pulling on the wool, only to look up and see the cat running out of the room with the ball of wool I was using in her mouth. I think she was telling me to take a break.

Ah, the whipping, not my favorite part of any rug project. Let's do the math... 8'+8'=16'=192"+(22"+22")=236."

I chose to do the whipping in black and tan. I hauled the mat down to my studio, where I had cleared off my 6' art table and started at the whipping, only to discover that the edge with my sewing machine was not all that straight. The solution for getting a straight edge was to count 19 burlap lines from the edge of the fabric backing, and mark the line with a needle and yarn. I bound the edge along that line, and then filled in the remaining background with the punch hook.

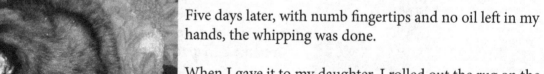

Five days later, with numb fingertips and no oil left in my hands, the whipping was done.

When I gave it to my daughter, I rolled out the rug on the floor and immediately Kitty jumped on. She rolled and stretched and was not giving up the rug she had watched over for the past month. My daughter laughed, saying she would have expected nothing less from me than a rug like this one. She loved the rug but was not sure if she wanted to put it on the floor. Then she walked on it and loved the feel of it under her feet. Her boyfriend came over and he laid down on it and found it warm and comfortable. The rug is waiting for them to paint their hallway.

You know how one thing leads to another... Kitty was so upset that I was giving her rug away that I designed a "bug in the rug" for her that she has nested in every night since I put it on the floor. Actually, she sat in it as I was hooking it!

GOING AU NATURAL

Jacob Sheep, natural colored Angora Goat
Edeldal Farm

Lincoln Photo by Dawn Lantz
Courtesy of Willow Creek Farm

Romney Photo by Al Schwider
Courtesy of The Pines Farm

Black Welsh Mountain
Photo by Mike Stann
Courtesy of Wild Wool
Farm

Did you know, there are over 100 breeds of sheep in the world? Sheep have been bred for centuries to produce different types of fleeces; some soft and silky, others rough and tough. They also come in a huge variety of natural colors; whites, grays, browns, blacks and reds.

This is one feature that yarn hookers can take advantage of, because you rarely can find the range of natural colors in fabric used in traditional rug hooking. Yarn takes us much closer to the source, and what a palette these natural colors can provide for rug hooking!

Navajo Photo by Karen Lobb
Courtesy of Bide a Wee Farm

13 Mile Lamb and Wool Company
www.lambandwool.com/yarn.htm

Bida a Wee Farm
www.bideaweefarm.com

Cascade Yarn
www.cascadeyarns.com/cascade-eco.asp

Blackberry Ridge
www.blackberry-ridge.com/specwool.htm

Toots le Blanc Border Leicester/Mohair
http://tootsleblanc.com/yarn.html

Toots le Blanc Jacob/Alpaca
http://tootsleblanc.com/yarn.html

These yarns are commercially spun from natural colors. I used these yarns to hook Block Party (page 68).

Opposite page:
Block Party 23.5"x30"
Designed and hooked by Judy Taylor

69

Forlorn Hope 23"x29"
Designed and hooked by Judy Taylor
Hooked with the handspun yarns on the opposite page

70

Sheep come in a variety of colors as well as fleece types. White, gray, brown, red and black, plus any combination of these colors can be achieved using only the natural colors. There are companies that feature commercially-spun yarns in natural colors (see the source guide on p, 69). Supplies and colors that are available commercially are somewhat limited, so here's where your new-best-friend-handspinner can really come in handy. You won't believe the shades and colors that you can get by going to the source, the sheep.

Just SOME of the colors you can get with handspun yarn! Breeds shown: Coopworth, Shetland, Suffolk, Karakul, Romney, Navajo, Jacob, Mohair, Corriedale, Icelandic, Herdwick, Masham, Manx Loaghtan, CVM, Finnish Landrace, Perendale, Alpaca, Swaledale, Lincoln, Border Leicester, Dorset Horn, Devon, Southdown, Texel, Wensleydale, Scottish Blackface, Falkland, Teeswater, Cormo, Norwegian Villsau, Cheviot, Black Welsh Mountain, Bluefaced Leicester, Grey Gotland, Poodle. (Yup, Poodle)

Celtic Dogs Rug 36.5"x24"
Designed and hooked by Judy Taylor
Handspun Jacob and Navajo yarn

あの日う美しい子

Good Morning My Beauty 9"x33.5"
Designed and hooked by Judy Taylor
Handspun Jacob yarn

Natural-colored wool can be dyed too, but there is something really classic about using the colors *au natural* in your rugs. They go beautifully together. I always think of pairing natural colored yarns with hardwood floors and overstuffed leather furniture. These colors never fade or go out of style. And it is nearly impossible to get this range of natural colors when hooking with fabric strips.

This palette is really only available for us yarn-hookers, the fabric folks have to dye their wool to get even close to these natural shades. If you've ever heard the expression "dyed in the wool," it refers to the quality and depth of color that you can get by spinning the colored wool, as opposed to dyeing the yarn or fabric after it is spun. If the yarn is "dyed in the wool," or a natural color, the color is consistent, even on the ends when the yarn is cut. This motto works for dyed wool as well as the natural-colored stuff. It is very distinctive.

Celtic Table Runner 13"x36"
Designed and hooked by Judy Taylor
Handspun Jacob and Icelandic yarn

73

Whale Rug 24"x30"
Designed and hooked by Judy Taylor
Handspun Jacob yarn

Above left: handspun yarns with smooth, lustrous color and texture. Above right: handspun yarns with rough, tweedy texture and muted in color

TEXTURE

As you get to experimenting with new yarns, you will find that there is a tremendous variety in texture available. Some yarns are lustrous, some more muted, and you can use these features to define and refine your details. Consider a rug design with all muted texture, when you bring in a bit of luster, you really bring out the detail. Handspun yarns are especially varied in texture, depending on the type of fleece. These yarns can sometimes diffuse the light, making the loops less prominent, so the design details come forward.

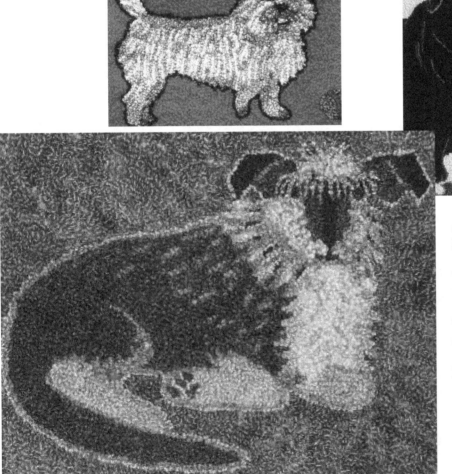

Close ups of dog portraits, hooked with handspun and commercial natural colors.

Top left: Tess (Finished rug measures 17.5"x30.5")

Top right: Penny, Pasha and Jezebel (Finished rug measures 21"x32.5")

Bottom left: Buster (Finished rug measures 17.5"x30.5")

Designed and hooked by Judy Taylor

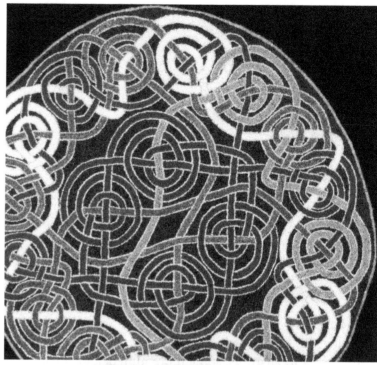

Top left: handspun Jacob Mat 14"x16"
Designed and hooked by Judy Taylor

Top right: close up of handspun Celtic Love Knot 48"x52"
Designed and hooked by Judy Taylor

Right: handspun Four Leaf Mat 8"x8"
Designed and hooked by Judy Taylor

Bottom left: handspun Celtic Triskellion Rug 38"x27"
Designed and hooked by Judy Taylor

Bottom right: handspun Jacob Iris Mat 9"x20"
Designed and hooked by Judy Taylor

Mady
Original photograph courtesy of
Walmart, Waterloo, Ontario
Wall hanging photography courtesy of
Portraits by Melissa, Ottawa, Ontario

After receiving a touchingly beautiful photograph of our granddaughter, Mady, and immediately knowing that it must be interpreted as a wall hanging in yarn, I set about making this inspiration take form.

I made two large (21"x17") copies of the photograph.

As the photograph was black and white, I decided to hook a monochromatic portrait (a double-first for me, as I tend to see/hook in vibrant colors, and had never hooked a portrait).

On one copy, I numbered the shaded areas from 1 to 8, from white to black. This would become my "working copy."

Going to my "stash" to see what might already be available, I found yarns ranging from white to black, including various types of yarn (some 100% wool, some combinations of wool and silk, synthetic, and yarns of various weights, like sock yarn and double knit). After sorting through the "stash," I had half of the shades I needed.

Time to shop! Luckily, I was able to purchase two more shades of grey, but I was still two shades short.

Time to bring out the dyepot! Desperately, I threw some of the black and grey yarn in a simmering pot of plain water, along with bleached and unbleached white yarn (Briggs & Little) to see what would happen. Simmer, simmer. Not being a chemist, I had no idea what to expect. Actually, I was anticipating "mud."

Magic! Wonderful surprise! As there were varying types and weights of yarn in the pot, the yarns gave up their "elements" to varying degrees and luckily, magically, the resulting shades of grey could be used for this project (and not set aside, as is sometimes the case, for future creations). The thought had crossed my mind that depending on the dyeing results, perhaps this piece would not be monochromatic!

I then transferred the basic outline and features from the second copy of the photograph onto red-dot material, taping the photograph with pinned on red-dot fabric onto a window so I could see all the design features clearly. I marked all my lines from the photo with a ball-point pen. As soon as I was sure I had all the necessary details marked, I put the red-dot material onto my linen, and transferred all the lines with a Sharpie pen.

Mady 27"x22"
Designed and hooked by
Bonnie Campbell
Framed by Malen of Ottowa

From there it was Happy Hooking! Hooking "by numbers," some "reverse hooking," use of longer strands of yarn to make Mady's hair look 3-dimensional, I then used silk yarn and silk ribbon with it's beautiful sheen for the flower that Mady is holding.

Beading and attaching a pearl necklace, as well as having the piece professionally framed, all resulted in my first portrait piece called "Mady."

Due to the timing of completion of the portrait, with pride, some tears and a smile, it was presented to Mady's great-grandmother on her 90th birthday.

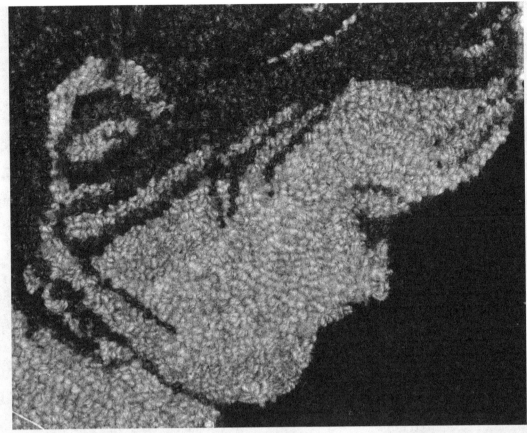

Close-up of face, showing the different shades of grey

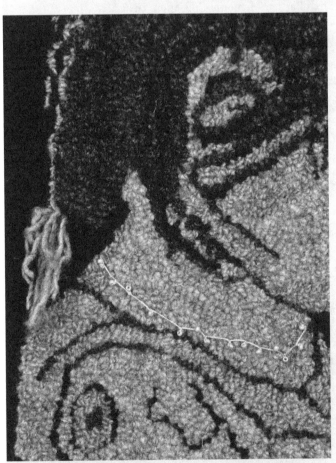

Close up of necklace. Beads by McBead Creations, Ottowa, Ontario

Close-up of the ponytail, with long strands for a 3-D effect

GETTING FINE DETAIL IN RUG HOOKING

In the late 19th century, a new movement was started among impressionist painters, called "pointillism." One of the most famous pointillist painters was Georges Seurat, whose life was dramatized in the Sondheim musical "Sunday In The Park With George." The pointillists were interested in the emerging science on color and how our eye perceives color. Instead of mixing colors on a palette, they painted colored dots on the canvas, and the different colored dots were blended by the viewer's eye. The effect of this style of painting was to create colors that seemed brighter. The paintings are often said to "shimmer," perhaps because each dot reflects light and color in its own way.

Our televisions, computers and printers operate in the same way today. Each image is presented on TV with a series of thousands of colored dots. When you think of it, a hooked rug is really made

A Sunday afternoon on the island of the Grande Jatte 1884. 1884-86. Oil on Canvas 81.75"x121.25"
Georges Seurat   Art Institute, Chicago, IL
Helen Birch Bartlett Memorial Collection, 1926.224.
Photo credit: Erich Lessing, Art Resource, NY

from thousands of dots, too. A detail in a hooked rug can be as small as just one loop.

Oriental designs are really challenging, because they are highly detailed, every loop shows, every loop counts. Designs are intricate, some are flowing and floral in style, some feature complex geometric patterns. Of course, real oriental patterns are made with very fine yarns, much finer than we normally hook with. So the challenge is how to create sharp detail in a hooked rug, and nothing demonstrates that better than Orientals.

While we usually hook with worsted-weight to bulky yarns, we can also incorporate much finer yarns in our designs, even as fine as embroidery thread! This takes some planning though, because these very fine yarns can be difficult to control in the hooking process. One strategy for getting those fine yarns incorporated is to hook around the detail, just as if the detail was already in place. If I hook in this way, I leave a pathway for the embroidery thread. It is much easier to bring in the thread if the surrounding loops are already in place.

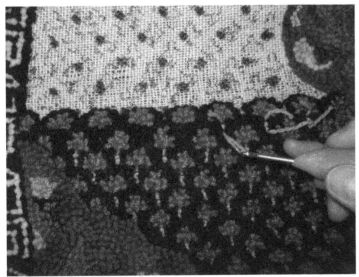

Close-up of Magic Carpet

The clover-leaves are hooked with a worsted weight yarn, the background is a medium-weight handspun, but hooking the stem with embroidery thread makes the whole pattern seem highly detailed. It is much easier to control the thread and get the loops even when the background yarn is already there to support them.

Sometimes when hooking with fine detail, it is not possible for me to hook around the detail like I did with the clover stems in Magic Carpet.

In the Lady Teasle rug, I couldn't start by hooking around the whiskers, because I would not have been able to find the pathways after hooking the background colors. In this case, I hooked the whiskers first, realizing that hooking with a fine yarn on its own would be hard to get right, but I did the best I could to place the whiskers with the handspun silk thread. I carefully hooked the backgrounds around the whiskers, then I unhooked the whiskers and re-hooked them through the pathways that were left in the background.

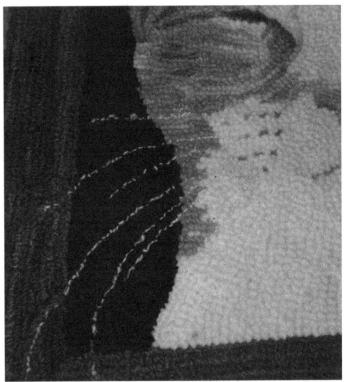

Above: Close-up of Lady Teasle showing the whiskers initially hooked and surrounded by the background yarn
Below: Whiskers rehooked with the background yarn in place

When I spend time in an Oriental rug shop, I am captivated by the intricate designs. I marvel at the details, how I can still make them out even standing 20 feet away. Notice how the luster in Lady Teasle's whiskers makes them stand out. This is partly because the whiskers are hooked with a fine yarn, but also because the yarn is silk. This is a technique that is used in many fine Oriental rugs too. Silk yarn is used in crucial details, which seen against a wool background, are surprisingly easy to make out from far away. While I was hooking Magic Carpet, I felt that the medallion in the center seemed to fade into the background. This often happens when you hook with two yarns, which when in their skeins seem quite different, but when hooked side by side, they seem to lack definition. When I hooked a silk yarn in between the medallion and the background, the medallion really popped out. The addition of the silk outline brought a sharpness to the overall effect.

There is a particular feature in Oriental rug design called "abrash." This refers to an unevenness in the dye colors, which in these rugs indicates that they were hand-dyed. If an Oriental rug has "abrash" it is highly valued because it is authentic to its region, hand-worked from start to finish, as opposed to rugs that are produced with commercially dyed yarns in huge quantities. You can create this "abrash" in your own designs by using the primitive dyeing method. For the Turkish Delight rug, I purposely dyed a variety of yarns in a variety of weights, and limited the water

Close-up of
Magic Carpet

Close-up of Turkish Delight

in the dyebath so I would have both a difference in texture within each color, but also the depth of color would vary as I hooked. By hooking with these variegated yarns in horizontal rows, it gave my rug the effect of a woven tapestry.

I really made use of fine yarns for outlining the details in Turkish Delight. The repeated design, called a "boteh" was easy to make sharp by outlining the shapes with a fine silk yarn. I outlined the diagonal sections with silk, as well as the center section, to set it off from the borders.

I have created many templates from traditional Oriental rug designs for you to experiment with (starting on page 169). You can combine them in any way you wish to create your own original designs.

Above left: Close-up of Turkish Delight. The red boteh on the lower left of the picture shows what it looked like before outlining. It really doesn't stand out against the black background. The red boteh to its right shows the silk outline added after hooking the background

Lower left: Persian Prayer Rug 32"x46"
Embroidery design, Isfahan (Iran), 17th c., private collection
Adapted and hooked by Margaret Arraj

Lower right: Chinese Carpet 33"x50"
Motifs from two Chinese carpets 19th c.
Adapted and hooked by Margaret Arraj

Featured Artist
Margaret Arraj
Northampton, MA

I take a very focused approach to rug hooking. I am primarily interested in furthering my own art, i.e., my color and design sensibilities through the actual making of rugs. I hook about three hours a day (one hour in the morning and two in the evening). I am now working on rug #100, not counting any small pieces. Everything else is secondary to this.

I specialize design-wise in historic and ethnic designs, because that is what attracts me. When I was first rug-hooking and wondering what designs I would use, I happened upon a poster book called "Art Nouveau Floral Designs." by Eugene Grasset. I was amazed at both the designs and the colors. This was the beginning of my journey into the decorative arts. Since then, I frequent libraries and used book stores, and more lately the internet, looking for designs that appeal to me.

Water Lilies 30"x40"
Art Nouveau floral design, private collection
Adapted and hooked by Margaret Arraj

I am wild about two-dimensional design. I love flat colors, and flat shapes as seen in the Arts and Crafts period, or Art Nouveau or primitive Early American, as well as Turkish art, Asian art, among others. Therefore I do not do fine shading. That is not to say that I do not use a number of closely related colors to express a motif.

Google images offer a seemingly endless view into the world collections. For example, I recently googled Oriental Rug Symbols. This led me to a design linked to a website filled with antique textiles. After enjoyably scrolling through many of these, I found a design from a Japanese kimono that captured my imagination. This will be my next rug.

English Vase 31"x38"
Mid-18th c. English embroidered pole screen
Metropolitan Museum of Art, private collection
Adapted and hooked by Margaret Arraj

Korean Cranes II 35"x37"
Rank badge, 1848-1888
Victoria and Albert Museum private collection
Adapted and hooked by Margaret Arraj

When I find a design, I like to do two things:

1. Try to determine if the design is copyright free. Copyright is complicated. That is one reason that I do historic designs because they are old enough to be in the public domain. There have been articles in Rug Hooking Magazine (2003) which deal with the copyright issue. Copyright-free designs are also readily available in Dover Publications design books. A person may also seek permission to do a rug from a publisher or artist. I have asked and received permission for my rug entitled Egyptian Tree.

2. I make from 2-6 small copies of the design I have chosen. From these I cut and paste repeating motifs, omitting motifs, adding or subtracting borders, etc. Sometimes I use a border and designs from different rugs. Someone who has good computer knowledge would be able to do this by computer. I like the hands-on feel of moving the pieces around. When I have a small copy to my liking I figure out the proportion of the rug and bring it to a copy shop to be enlarged. You need a copy shop that can do copies 36" wide.

I maintain a list of designs I have found that may be potential rugs. But choosing is a dance between the design and where I am. Sometimes the choice is made because of a color palette I have in mind. But all in all, I regard the design process of rug hooking very important. After the technique of hooking is learned, rug hooking is all about design and color. The finished product will only be as good as these.

I am rather a purist when it comes to the yarn I use. My studio is filled with about 90% medium-weight 2 or 3-ply rug wool yarn. The rest might be bulky, and some single-ply weaving yarns. I have hooked with handspun yarns, mohair, etc., but my favorite is 3-ply medium weight New Zealand rug wool yarn. Since most of it comes on spools as remnants from carpet factories, I dye plenty of yarn to get the colors I want.

I use a Puritan frame (which I love), a Moshimer hook, size M, and hook the same way strip hookers hook. Of course there are differences between hooking strips and yarn. The actual experience of hooking with yarn will be the best teacher.

Iranian Prayer Rug, 1830's-1840's
Adapted and hooked by Martgaret Arraj

85

Persian Peace Garden 43"x62"
Prayer cloth of Shah Abbas, Isfahan (Iran) 17th c.
Private collection
Adapted and hooked by Margaret Arraj

Uzbek Sunflower 27.5"x44"
Central Asian embroidery 17th-18th c.
Adapted and hooked by Margaret Arraj

Courthouse Rug 20"x47"
Facade of the Hampshire County Courthouse,
Northampton, MA, 1884
Adapted and hooked by Margaret Arraj

Glorious Garden 32.5"x56"
Source: an antique woven rug remnant
Adapted and hooked by Margaret Arraj

Isis 28"x45"
Art Nouveau wallpaper, C.F.A. Voysey,
1893, private collection
Adapted and hooked by Margaret Arraj

The White Garden 33"x38"
19th century Aesthetic
Movement upholstery
Adapted and hooked by
Margaret Arraj

You can view Margaret's rugs at
www.millriverrugs.com

Simply Suzani 43"x48"
Source: 19th c. Suzani rug motifs
Adapted and hooked by Margaret Arraj

Ocean 26"x57"
Asiatic water design
Adapted and hooked by Margaret Arraj

Unfinished Business

Repair and refinishing of old rugs

Figure 1: Close up of the Pinwheel Rug, with a small amount of yarn pulled up

One of the best things about hand hooked rugs is how easy they are to repair. Many people balk at the idea of putting these rugs on the floor, but if you keep a well-made hooked rug for a while, you come to find how durable they are, and if they should ever get stained or damaged, it is easy as pie to fix them.

The most common issue for hooked rugs is the occasional loop that gets snagged. In this Pinwheel rug, you can see a little of the light pink yarn in the pinwheel has been pulled up. Nothing could be easier. I just turned the rug over and rehooked the yarn.

Figure 2: Same section of the rug, with the yarn pulled through to the back for re-hooking

91

Figure 3: Rehooked area from the back side

Figure 4: The rehooked area from the front

Sometimes the backing is damaged as well, and needs to be replaced before re-hooking. In the rug on page 91, a dog chewed the rug, and ate the backing and yarn as well! No need to throw out the rug (or the dog!) because this too can easily be repaired.

For this rug, I unhooked the area around the damage, until I got to healthy backing. I sewed a new piece of backing to the old, tacking down all of the original backing. Then I re-hooked through both layers with new yarn. This rug was relatively new, so the colors were not faded, so I was able use yarn from my stash. When you look at this rug from the top, you cannot see where the damage took place. If you examine the back, you can see the outlines of the patched backing.

92

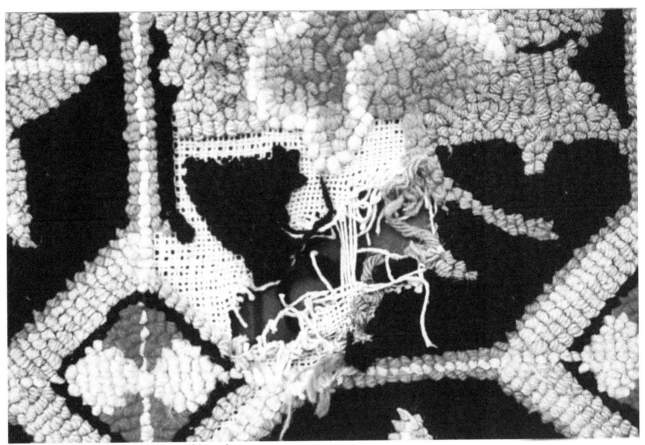

Figure 5: Close up of a rug chewed by a dog

Figure 6: Same rug after repair

93

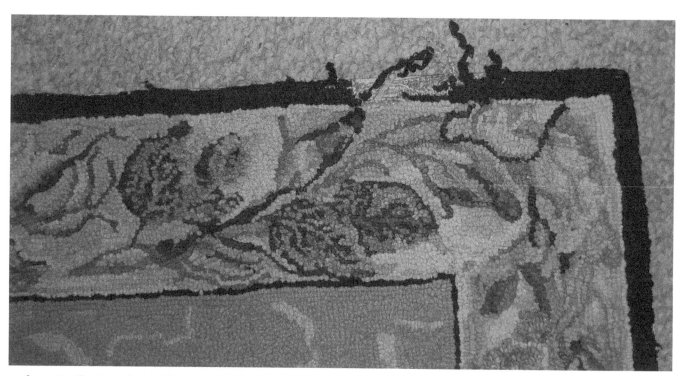

figure 7: Close up of a 1940's era rug that had a worn-out edge, so some of the yarn was pulling out

Figure 8: Same rug after rehooking the border, with a bound edge to protect from future damage

Another frequent repair issue for old rugs comes when the edges are not bound. (See basic rug hooking instructions, starting on p. 182) The first place to wear out on a hooked rug is the edge, so often old rugs need to be patched and rehooked along the edge.

I always recommend binding the edge of new rugs, because it is so effective in protecting the rug from wear and tear. If you have an old rug without a bound edge (most of the older rugs don't have bound edges), you can extend the life of your rug, just by binding it now, before the backing gets damaged.

But what if the damage has already occurred? No problem. Just as with the rug in Figure 7, the process of repairing a damaged edge is to undo the hem and unhook the yarn (or fabric strips) until you get to healthy backing. Add a patch to the damaged area, sewing it down to the old backing, then re-hook through both layers. The rug in Figure 7 had typical wear along the edges, so when I got the border patched and re-hooked, I bound the edge, then completed the hem. Now it can be enjoyed for many more years to come.

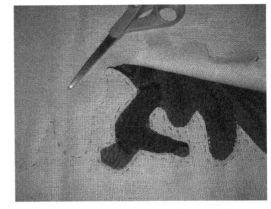

Figure 9: Cutting away patch after it has been tacked down (view from the back)

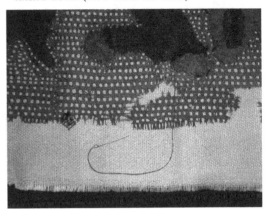

Figure 10: Tacking down the ragged edges of the original backing (view from the front)

Figure 11: Rehooking through both the original backing and the patch

Figure 12: The leaf rug with the damaged areas exposed (view from the back)

Figure 13: With all of the black outer background unhooked, this is a shot of the rug from
the front, with the patch sewn in

This old rug had extensive damage all around the edges. I unhooked the damaged spots, and the owner of the
rug chose to have me unhook the entire black border, and put in one large patch to support the whole exterior
of the design. I tacked a large piece of burlap to the back of the rug, and cut away the center (figure 9). I then
tacked the whole original backing to the patch, especially sewing down the ragged edges (figure 10),

Figure 14: The patch sewn in place before rehooking (view from the back)

Figure 15: The black border, rehooked with new yarn before hemming

Figure 16: View from the back of the finished rug. All of the damaged spots have been patched and rehooked, the edge has been bound and hemmed

Figure 17: Close up of the finished edge

Figure 19: Close-up of damaged rug, before adding the patch (view from the back)

Figure 20: Same section, repaired (front view)

so I could rehook through both layers (figure 11). I rehooked the design elements with handspun yarn and yarn from my stash. Then I bound the edge, so the finished rug can now be enjoyed for many years to come.

After repairing the rug, I gave it a simple hand cleaning. I had one pan of water with a splash of liquid laundry detergent and a bit of vinegar, and another pan of plain water. I dipped my rag into the soapy pot and in a circular motion, scrubbed the top of the rug. After washing a section, I put a clean rag into the plain water and rinsed it, section by section. I repeated this whole process on the back side of the rug, then left it where it could air dry. It is surprising how much you can brighten up a rug by this simple cleaning method.

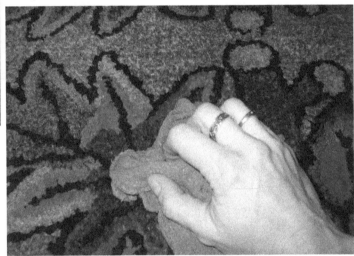

Figure 18: Washing the rug

Jo's Rug 33.5"x21"
Courtesy of Jo Vetter

This is an unfinished rug that my friend Jo found in her mom's attic.

To view the step-by-step process to refurbish this old gem, visit www.littlehouserugs.com/unfinished-biz-sept-2014.html

Here is another example of a rug repair. I unhooked the damaged edge of the Cocker Spaniel rug, until I got down to healthy backing. I patched and rehooked the edge, then I added hem tape all around the edge, so I would have enough to bind the edge. The original rug had fringe, so I added it to the repaired rug.

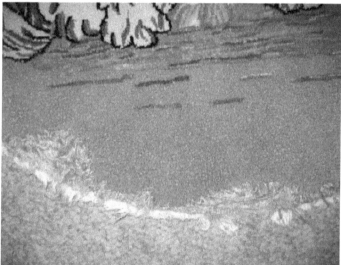

Top left: A 1940's era rug with a damaged edge

Left: Close-up of the damaged edge

Bottom left: View of the rug after all of the yarn had been removed from the edge, until I got to healthy backing

Bottom right: I added hem tape to the burlap edge, so I could bind the edge

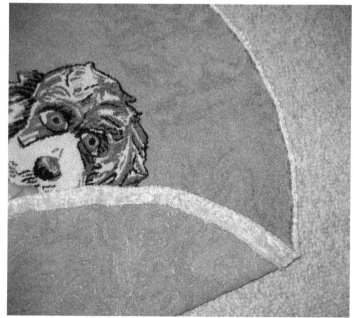

Cocker Spaniel Rug finished. I bound the edge with a matching pink yarn, then I added fringe, to restore the rug to its original look

For every rug hooker in this world, (and every rug hooker that ever was in this world), there is an unfinished rug. Or in my case, at this point, five unfinished rugs. If the lord should call me today, someone else will inherit my unfinished projects. What if my children have no interest in finishing them? This is quite a dilemma for many people.

You can finish these old rugs, using the techniques that you have learned in this book.

I finished this lovely runner, using as much as I possibly could of the original hooking. I was able to finish the scroll work, blending in my yarn to match the colors, such that you can't tell the difference between the old and the new hooking. But try as I might, I couldn't match the center purple section. Every yarn that I tried looked too different, so we decided to create a medallion in the center. I moved the original fabric strips around to center them on the runner, then I hooked a border around the medallion and filled in behind it with a darker purple yarn.

Figure 28: An unfinished runner

Figure 29: Finished runner

Figure 26: An unfinished oriental geometric design

Figure 27: Same rug, finished

I didn't need to spin or dye any yarn to finish this rug. I was able to find all the colors I needed using my stash, and a trip to the yarn store. Yarn is so versatile and available in such an amazing array of colors, it is perfect for finishing these unfinished gems.

Figure 30: An old rug of an Irish Terrier

Figure 31: All of the background yarn removed

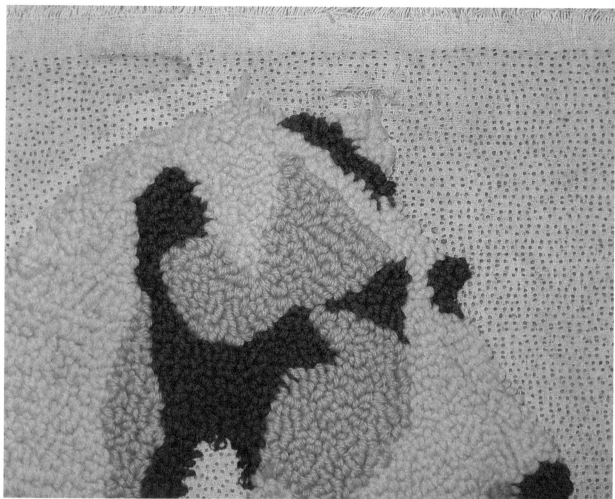

Figure 32: There was a small hole in the backing, above the dog's head

Figure 33: I patched the hole before rehooking the background

Perhaps you would like to spruce up an old rug, to keep it in the style of your current home. Hooked rugs are nothing if not versatile! This Irish Terrier rug had a lovely dog, but I was not crazy about the bright green background.

I picked out all of the green background. I noticed a small hole above the dog's head, which I patched, but other than that, the backing was in very good shape. I drew out a checkerboard pattern and added the words "Good Dog." I sewed some hem tape around the perimeter, because I needed more backing to do the hem.

I used a hand-dyed yarn that had a lot of color variation. I hooked the background in a "basket weave" pattern.

106

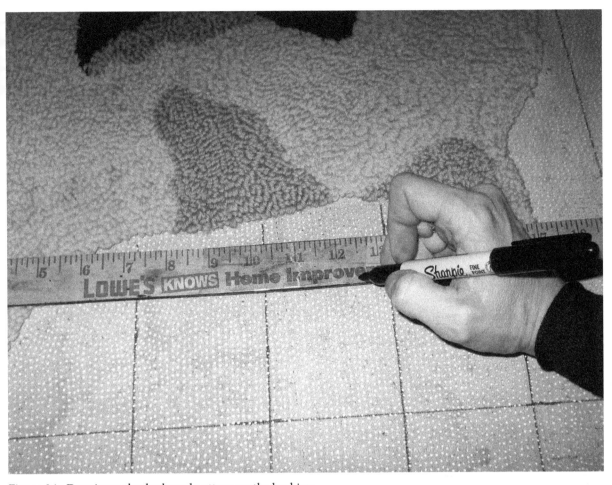

Figure 34: Drawing a checkerboard pattern on the backing

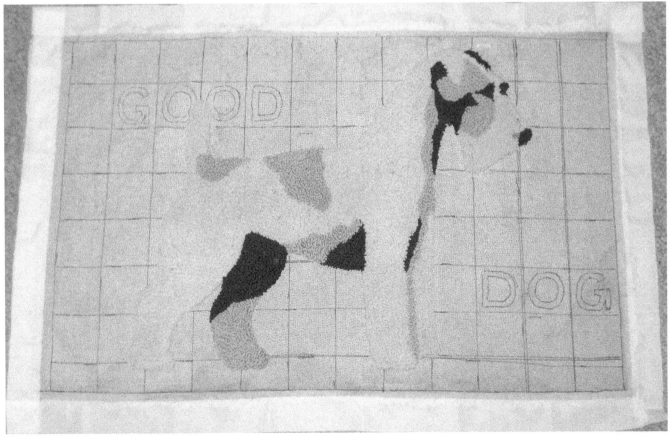

Figure 35: Hem tape was added to the edge, to allow for binding

Figure 36: Refurbished rug (opposite page)

HOOKED RUG. MR. AND MRS. W. T. GUILD. EAST BEACH. LONG BEACH. MISS.

Antique postcards featuring hooked rugs

COPYRIGHT BY H. MARSHALL GARDINER, NANTUCKET, MASS.

1016   LIVING ROOM. JETHRO COFFIN HOUSE 1686, NANTUCKET, MASS.

109

Featured Artist
Steve Grappe
Rockport, Texas

This is an image of contrast, with soothing green colored pads and sharp needles ready to inflict pain to the unwary. My plan was to, as much as the medium of yarn punching allowed, accurately duplicate the cactus in a natural green color, but infuse a little bit of colored highlight to add interest to the plain green pads. When you create rugs, you realize that the background, or the negative space, is just as important as the main design component itself. I added curving lines and color variation to the background sky blue color to give it movement.

Prickly Pear Cactus 18"x25" Designed and hooked by Steve Grappe

I have always liked rugs. They're so colorful and practical and feel good under your bare feet. I learned to hook rugs about four years ago and then soon switched to rug punching with yarn because it seemed faster. Very quickly I realized that all the rug patterns and kits out there were not for me. Most of them were in the primitive style, or they were of cute bunnies or pumpkins or other patterns that did not work for me. So, out of necessity I began to design my own rug patterns.

That's no big deal to an artist, because, after all, that's what they do. They make art out of the ordinary. However in my case, that was a tall order because I was just a guy who liked rugs. I couldn't draw. I didn't know the first thing about composition, color theory or style. I just knew what I liked and didn't like. It seemed I disliked more than I liked, but that somehow gave me a style all my own.

To work around my lack of drawing ability, I used my camera to take photos of images that looked artistic and easy to make into a rug. If the design needed to be simplified, it was easy to remove some of the elements. Next I used a computer to resize the image to the dimensions of the finished rug. In essence I created a design, not from an artist's canvas, but from a "work-around" of my inability to draw.

However, progressing from the initial photo to the finished rug is not a simple straight line "point A to point B" process. Something happens somewhere in the middle and the artistic process takes over. Colors get bolder, other design elements are added, and the final rug emerges from a process that is often messy, confusing and wonderful.

110

I sometimes feel like I am an unwelcome guest at an artist's party. But then, art is not created just from a blank canvas. Art is also about finding artistic designs in everyday life and translating them into a craft which either interprets the design or expands its original intent.

If I had to describe my color style, I would simply say it is bold, saturated and colorful. I love bright colors in my rugs. Anything less is just dull and uninspiring. When I first started making rugs, I did not see the need to dye my own yarn. After all, you could buy many colors of pre-dyed yarn. I thought dyeing was too messy and scientific for a simple rug artisan. Well I soon learned that I had to rethink my decision to steer away from the dye pot. In order to get those subtle color changes needed for shading and artistic expression, you have to dye your own yarn in the colors you want.

When I first began to dye I bought the colors I wanted and began to amass an expensive collection of premixed dyes. I realized I didn't have the shelf space or the budget to stock a full palette of colors, so I began to mix colors based on the three primaries and black. I was fortunate to find a book by Susan Rex called Complex Colors : Color Mixing for Acid Fast Dyes. Her system uses Cyan, Magenta, black and Yellow to mix all the secondary and tertiary colors needed for a rug artisan's palette. Following her system almost any color can be mixed using a "parts" or "percentage" measuring system based on dye powder weight or volume.

Here is my back yard photo which served as my inspiration.

Party Line 36"x29" Designed and hooked by Steve Grappe

I wanted to create a design using an image of birds on a wire, and looked at my back yard for inspiration. I took a photo of my back yard electrical utility pole against the sky and cropped it to my liking. The photo had all the elements I needed - sky, clouds, trees, birds, the utility pole with wires and insulators.

Here is where the interpretation begins. Most of what I did followed the design of the photo. However, I added more birds to the wire and in the sky and deleted some wires to simplify the design. In picking my colors I began with the reds, oranges and yellows to jazz up the plain brown of the pole. The blue sky and the mauve gray clouds just kind of followed.

The back porch photo that inspired the rug.

This rug is a vacation memento of a trip to New Orleans. How best to remember a great trip than a rug depicting a photo of a favorite spot. This rug design is of a back porch with the Trumpet Vines and Hibiscus Flower set against the richly colored siding of the old house. Again, I chose to exaggerate the hue and saturation of the colors.

Trumpet Vines at the Back Door 22"x28"
Designed and hooked by Steve Grappe

I decide on my colors one or two at a time and throw the yarn into the pot. Once I have those first few colors punched into the rug backing, it is easy to keep adding colors that go with them. I don't always try for a solid color, sometimes I over dye or keep some of the skein out of the pot to get a variegated look. Dyeing is very enjoyable and rewarding to see your natural wool yarn come alive with vibrant color that you created.

These are a few examples of my rugs, and my process to go from an idea, to a photo, to a color palette, to a finished rug. There is art in everyday life, and it is up to the rug artisan to find it, capture it, interpret it and make it into a rug. All my rugs are punched onto a base of Monks Cloth using my hand dyed wool yarn.

If you are looking to design your own rugs, be sure you like the subject matter, because you will spend a lot of time hooking or punching the rug. You can turn a plain photograph or other image into an awesome rug. Pick something that is simple in design, as a complex design does not translate well into a rug. Don't try for realism and save room for the artist in you to interpret what you see. Don't be afraid to crank up the color a notch to make it eye catching. I bet you will be pleased with your own design and your finished rug.

Eye Stripe Surgeon Fish 19"x19"
Designed and hooked by Steve
Grappe

This fish rug began as a photo of a
Surgeon Fish that had very subtle
markings. I cropped out most of
the fish body leaving only the fish
head. I bolded the markings and
added my own color scheme. With
the fish body being a sky blue, I
added olive green and patches of
yellow to the markings. The water
background looked good in purple
to give contrast to the blue. My
intent was to make the distinctive
body markings the primary focus
of the rug.

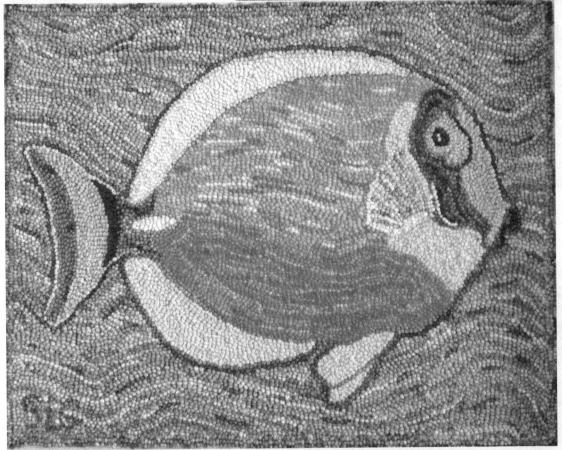

The Blue Tang fish is very
adaptable as a rug design.
It has distinct color areas
of the body, so staying
close to the natural design
and coloration of the fish
was very easy to do. I
decided to add a maroon
outline to define it better
from the background.

Powder Blue Tang Fish 21"x28"
Designed and hooked by Steve Grappe

113

Priscilla Turner Rug Guild

fine handcraft...

FOR TODAY'S SUCCESSFUL DECORATING

Priscilla Turner Hooked Rugs ... perfect complement to your handloomed fabrics, finest wallpaper, and custom-blended paints. Select from countless patterns, and exclusive pattern combinations. Priscilla Turner rugs are *individually hooked*. Your very personal taste in color, shape, design, is expressed with talent and imaginative freshness ... in the deep-piled luxury of 100% virgin wool.

A. *Stair Treads, Pattern 213 (113), Green. Also available in Black, Wine, Brown.*

B. *Pinewood Texture, Wood Rose. Example of custom rug hooking to decorator specification.*

C. *Pattern 203 (320) in 4' x 6', Beige. Also available in Black, Green, Blue.*

D. *Pattern 120 in 6' x 9', Black.*

E. *Pattern 123 (455) in 9' x 12', Black. Also available in Wine, Green, Brown.*

F. *Pattern 216 (615) in 4' x 6', Brown. Also available in Green, Wine, Black, Royal Blue.*

Standard room sizes (from 2' x 3' to 12' x 20') are available. Also special sizes and shapes hooked to exact decorator specifications.

Send for color folio! Mail 10c, with your name and address, for illustrated folder and name of nearest dealer. Address: Dept. C-10, Priscilla Turner Rug Guild, Turner, Maine.

LOOK FOR THIS LABEL

The personal autograph of the "hooker" is attached to every Priscilla Turner Rug.

Priscilla Turner
Rug Guild
TURNER, MAINE

House Beautiful ad
October, 1953

Opposite page: Priscilla Turner Rug 23"x33"
Photo courtesy of Richard and Judy Dennis
Note: This rug is featured in the magazine ad shown on this page

Help wanted, female experienced
rug hookers. Good pay.
Priscilla Turner Rug Guild.
Turner, Maine, Phone 41 after 6pm.

Lewiston Everning Journal
January 22, 1918

WANTED
Girls and women on Priscilla Turner rugs.
No school girls or vacationists.
Only those desiring steady
employment. Good pay while learning.
Call in person at the rug factory in
Turner, Maine. Tel. 25-2

Lewiston Daily Sun
July 15, 1924

The Priscilla Turner Rug Guild is a company that operated from the 1920's to the 1980's in Turner, Maine. They hooked rugs with yarn, and sold them commercially all over the East Coast and beyond. The company was clearly very proud of the careful hand work of their artists, who made each rug from start to finish. Every Priscilla Turner rug had a tag attached, to which the rug hooker signed her name. I find this wonderful and amazing that a company would promote the artist on the tag. I also love the tag because relatively few old rugs have any name or date at all. These distinctive tags make the Priscilla Turner rugs all the more unique.

They had a large catalog of designs to choose from, and they also welcomed custom orders. A rug was even made in 1988 for the White House, a 9'x12' rug of the Presidential Seal.

Many Priscilla Turner rugs are still in use, and often are seen at auctions and antique stores. The company is part of the rich story of rug hooking in North America. Most of the people who worked in the factory have now passed on, and it is left to us to remember this unique company and all of its beautiful creations.

Good morning:

I am the daughter of the late Phyllis M. Martin, formerly of North Turner and later years Springfield, VT. My mother hooked beautiful rugs at Priscilla Turner for many years. I actually went with Mom to work each day (employees were allowed to bring a child, although I don't remember very many who did). This was before I started school, of course. I remember very well the following people who worked there: Ernie (he was like a Grandpa) who did maintenance on the machines that the women hooked the rugs with, and Kitty, who did the patterns for the rugs. The second floor is where all the frames for the rugs were. I believe the third floor was where all the spools of yarn were kept and the women would holler up a number of the yarn through an opening in the floor and I was allowed to gather the specific number of yarn and drop it in the box to them. I want to say Carolyn Libby was the yarn keeper.

I wish I could remember the name of the owner because I was the only child that he allowed in the showroom where all the completed rugs were and I would have my nap every afternoon! He never cared which rug I slept on. The very first time I fell asleep, Mom came to get me and the owner said to leave me there, that I was not doing any harm (of course, I had to remove my shoes). I guess you could say I had the run of the place so to speak. I was well behaved and the owner knew that.

I remember Mom bent over this large steel frame hooking away on the rug, no wonder she had back trouble in later years. She did beautiful work which she was praised for several times. I would give anything to have a rug with my Mom's name on the label. I can remember how beautiful her rugs were. She hooked more than one 9'x12' rug during her time there. Every week, a small group would get into someone's car and go to the Lone Pine on RT 4 for lunch. They had the best pepper steak sandwich and their homemade strawberry pie, served in the green soup bowl, was to die for. (Continued on page 117)

I would estimate Mom worked there from late forties to the middle fifties. We moved to Lewiston when I was in the sixth grade, so I was approximately 11-12 years of age. I was born in February, 1944. I remember four women, including my Mom, who hooked the rugs on the second floor. Of course, the frames were so large that I would estimate maybe 6 women could have been on the second floor. As I remember, the second floor was the only floor for assembling the rugs. I couldn't begin to even estimate the number of rugs Mom made. Of course, the smaller ones went quickly, but the big 9'x12' must have taken much longer. I remember all the vivid colors, they were just beautiful. Hopefully someone will contact you with more info. I wish you the best on researching your new book.

Sandie Fox
Lewiston, ME

Excerpt from an article about Leota Seward

Recalling the years past, the hardy senior describes a diverse job record. In the early '40's she joined the seasonal work crew at the Burnham-Morrill canning factory in North Turner. Seeking a full-time job, she later went to Priscilla Turner Rug Factory where she worked as a rug hooker for 20 years. Those were prosperous days for Priscilla Turner, with the handhooked rugs shipped all over the country. It was hard work for the women, bent long hours over the rug frames, and they took much pride in their skill.

When they sold the farm in 1952, they moved to Turner Village and for a couple of years they operated a small store. "I didn't like working in the store," Leota remembers, "so I kept on hooking rugs." In 1963, she put down the hooking machine and went home to care for her aging parents.

Sun Journal October 26, 1995

PRISCILLIA TURNER RUG FACTORY

First known as DeForest Products Company, Priscilla Turner Rug Factory, founded in 1923, employed many townspeople until it moved out of town in 1969. Their colorful hand hooked rugs were shipped all over the northeastern United States. The towering water tank provided the best fire protection for many years. Insert shows worker Leota Seaward who celebrated her 100th birthday in 2010.

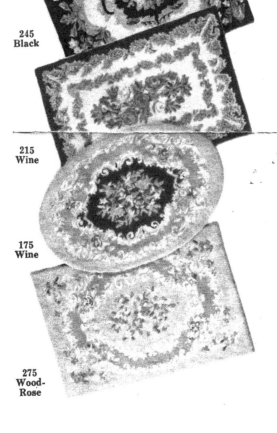

140 Green

115 Black

203 (320) Green

245 Black

215 Wine

175 Wine

275 Wood-Rose

Rugs to the left on this page are illustrated in size 4 feet by 6 feet. Other sizes are scaled in artistic proportion. Example — see the 6' x 9' and 9' x 12' illustrations. As in any hand made rug, all sizes are approximate.

For simpler identification, oblong or rectangular patterns are now numbered in the 200 series and their oval counterparts in the 100 series. This has necessitated renumbering some designs — in such cases the former number is shown in brackets immediately following the new number.

With the exception of 203(320) and 213(113), all designs are available in oval shape as well as oblong.

Priscilla Turner Hooked Rugs can be made in any length and up to 21 ft. wide . . . and in solid colors, broadloom type, known as Priscilla Turner "Shell Hook."

You can select almost any type or shape — welcome mat, hearth or scatter rugs; living room, dining room, den or bedroom rugs — long-life rugs to meet any of your floor covering needs.

These illustrations, created thru the finest medium of photography and printing, are, in general, true replicas of original rugs. Variations in ink and variations in shades of yarn from one dye lot to another preclude exact matching of colors.

When you see these beautiful rugs . . foot — you sense immediately the discern . . . the pride of the conscientious craft joins quality to beauty.

Knowing this . . . proud of the old N . . . proud too of their skill . . . each personally signs the label attached to you

Always look for the label which gua: scoured in American Mills, clean as the 1

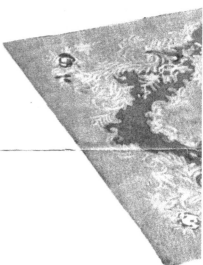

H ere are rugs that "fit in" anyw . . . add gaily colored accents or

Here are rugs that give you whose creation by the oldest hool

Here are rugs so varied in c need . . . that you can choose 1 mirror your own tastes . . . and e thoughtfulness you put into your

Here is the TEXTURE y only in Priscilla Turner hooked better can you express "The An

118

...ke a family heirloom

...when you feel them — by touch or under
...g taste fulfilled in their designs and colors
...an in making a product that genuinely

...v England tradition they are perpetuating
...aker of a Priscilla Turner hooked rug
...rug.

...tees you the finest virgin wool, spun and
...rs in a baby's garment.

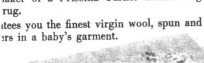

275 Blue
In Size 6' x 9'

*Illustrated above: Hearth Mats —
Welcome Mat. Available in Ground
Colors of Beige, Black, Wine,
Brown and Dark Green. Size: Ap-
prox. 19" x 38"*

...ere in your home . . . blend harmoniously with any decor
...hly subdued tones to any room.

...rue luxury to "fit in" with any family's budget . . . rugs
...d rug Guild assures you many years of use and beauty.

...ign and shape and size . . . so adaptable to your every

...se that truly
...ress the extra
...me planning.

...want, found
...gs . . . How
...rican Style"?

221 (310) Green
In Size 6' x 9'

115 Brown
In Size 9' x 12'

Magazine ad
Courtesy of the Turner Historical Museum

119

Priscilla Turner Rug 34"x58"
(can't read the name of the hooker or the design on the tag)

Priscilla Turner Rug   36"x18"
Hooked by Esther Dow. Stock #54 or 5A
Courtesy of Dianne Maillet, Athens, TN
This rug is featured on the magazine ad on page 119

Priscilla Turner Guild Rug ca. 1930's

I worked at the rug shop, off and on, for quite a few years. The first time I worked there was in 1948. I worked in the finishing department. We did repairs, such as checking for imperfections, pressing the rugs, hemming them and adding the tags. I quit when I got married, but then returned a few years later and learned to hook rugs. It was piece work. There were a lot of folks working there at the time. I don't recall exactly, but I'd say there were around 12 or 14 ladies doing the hooking, 6 or 7 men working in the machine shop and handling the backing on the frames and so forth. 6 or 8 ladies in the finishing department.

I used to take my children to work with me. I worked until I had to change to a night shift because of convenience somewhere else. I went back to the rug shop a few years later. They added a big machine to turn out a more carpet-like product and I worked on that machine. Also, at one time I worked on the yarn winder.

I am sure we had good times and bad. Sometimes there were fights--- always patched up. Sometimes, when on piece work, we always felt there was favoritism. Some patterns were easier than others.

I say we had it pretty good! We set our own hours more or less, and we could take our kids with us and so forth. Good friendships were formed also. One time Betty Durgin, Irene Durgin and I went to Yarmough, Maine, to repair a rug. It was in a mansion. My last year there was 1972.

Vivian Russell Mancine, Rug Hooker
Turner, Maine

121

Nestled in the New England village of Turner, Maine, is a three story shop, the home of "Priscilla Turner Rugs." The whistle would blow at 7 am, 12 noon, and pm. However, unlike many factories of the time, this one was very family oriented. There were approximately 50-60 employees, all women except for 6 or 7 men. Employees were allowed to bring their children who were three years old or older, to work with them. Since my grandmother, Viola Nickerson, my mother, Martha Durgin and my Aunt Lillian Leadbetter were all hookers there, I was one of those children. There was no child labor there, we played throughout the factory all morning. After lunch, we were encouraged to try to take a nap in the makeshift hammocks of canvas that were strung on the frames near where our mothers were hooking. A lot of mornings were spent visiting with the workers in all the departments. I can still recall all the people, their names and their jobs.

The rug starts in the pattern room on the first floor. Cincy would draw the pictures-- usually the traditional floral designs and sometimes custom-ordered designs to match the decor of someone's home or business. Once even the eagle insignia for the rug that was made for the Oval Office in the White House. Once the drawing was complete, it would be traced by a motorized little wheel that had very sharp points that put little holes in the brown paper-- thus creating a pattern. The pattern would be secured to a large piece of backing, a canvas-like material that was stretched tightly on the floor. Tom or Woody would heavily paint the pattern with a black ink that would seep through the backing. Once dried, the backing would be transported to the second floor, where Gus would load the frame.

Way up on the third floor was a winding machine where Carolyn would wind the yarn around cardboard cones by colors. The colors were all numbered instead of named. It was very important to have the exact shades to portray the designs for each traditional rug and to make samples for all custom-made rugs.

Now the backing is on the frame and the yarn is ready! We're almost ready to hook. The hooker on the second floor goes to the wooden dumb waiter operated by ropes-- rings the bell and Ernie or Ray will send up that hooker's machine. Each hooker's machine was set up to accommodate the individual hooker--- sort of like knitting, not everyone has the same tension. The machine was electric and weighed about 12 pounds. It looked like the old hand-turned egg beaters only bigger, with a motor on top and a little steering wheel toward the bottom that had a needle in the middle that went up and down. Now the hooker rings Carolyn on the third floor and tells her the number yarn needed to do the job-- down it comes on the dumb waiter. I always wanted a ride in the dumb waiter but it wasn't allowed. To the frame we go.

The frame was a little more than waist high, made of steel pipes, both ends had nails sticking up and one end had a cog wheel to tighten the backing and keep it taut. You thread the machine with a color and you lean over the frame, holding the machine upright you press the clutch that controls the speed. You turn the little wheel that has the needle pumping up and down, and proceed to fill in all the areas that call for the color you have threaded. You continue on with the next color, and the next, until the rug is finished.

My back aches already just thinking about it-- my mother did this for over 30 years! She worked through many changes in ownership and locations, as did several other dedicated hookers. Most of them, like my mother, knew more about making the rugs than did the new owners. They new owners were appreciative of the experienced hooker's knowledge.

The hooked rug would now be taken back to the first floor and spread out on large tables where the finishers, Peggy, Ada, Evelyn and Vivian, to name a few, would inspect and correct any imperfections with a hand-held hook. Now the edges would be hemmed and the famous silk tag, signed by the hooker, would be sewn in the hem.

One more step-- it had to be steam pressed. This machine looked like a big sandwich toaster, four feet by eight feet, and when they brought the cover down there was a large swoosh sound and the steam poured out. Finally, the rug is displayed in the showroom, rolled up and wrapped in brown paper and shipped away. All of this, we were exposed to and I do not recall any child ever having an injury.

Lana Obie
Turner, Maine

The two rugs above were featured
in a promotional book from the
Priscilla Turner Rug Guild

Priscilla Turner Rug 46"x22"(can't read the name of the hooker or the design
on the tag)

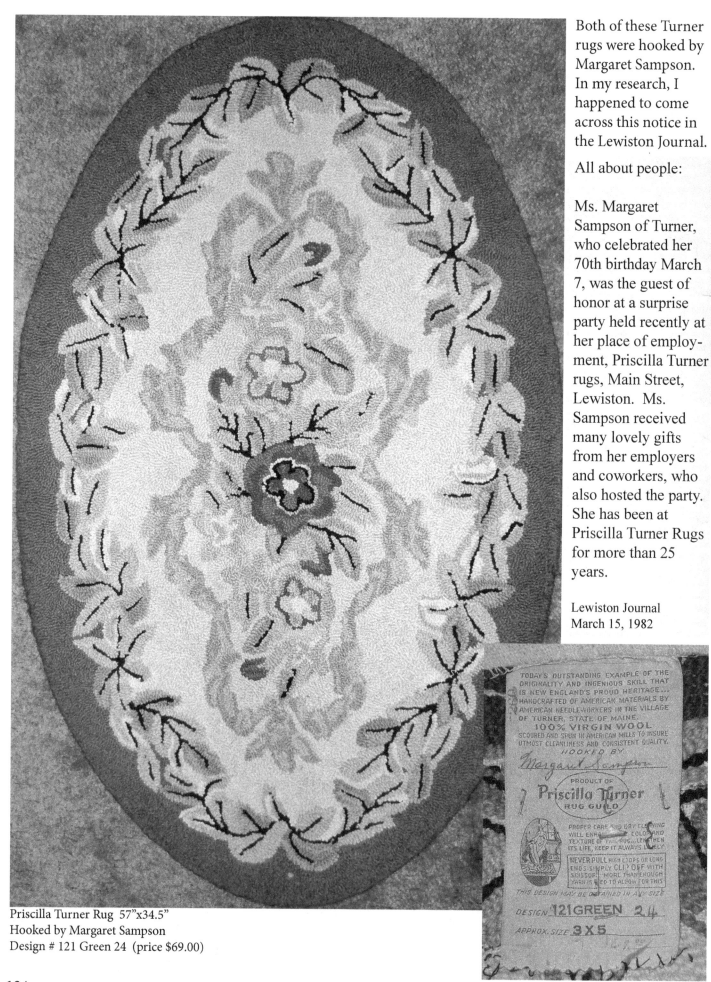

Both of these Turner rugs were hooked by Margaret Sampson. In my research, I happened to come across this notice in the Lewiston Journal.

All about people:

Ms. Margaret Sampson of Turner, who celebrated her 70th birthday March 7, was the guest of honor at a surprise party held recently at her place of employment, Priscilla Turner rugs, Main Street, Lewiston. Ms. Sampson received many lovely gifts from her employers and coworkers, who also hosted the party. She has been at Priscilla Turner Rugs for more than 25 years.

Lewiston Journal
March 15, 1982

Priscilla Turner Rug 57"x34.5"
Hooked by Margaret Sampson
Design # 121 Green 24 (price $69.00)

124

Priscilla Turner Rugs, individually hooked of luxurious, deep-piled 100% virgin wool-- are available in countless authentic patterns, or will be hooked-to-order in the shape and colors of your choice. For a lifetime, you'll love Priscilla Turner Rugs--- signed by the hooker, who made them for you alone.
Long and Company

The Portsmouth Times
April 23, 1955

Priscilla Turner Rug 58"x34.5"
Hooked by Margaret Sampson
Design # 120 Black 60 (price $69.00)

125

PRISCILLA TURNER HOOKED RUGS

IN THE

QUAINT DESIGNS

AND

RICH COLORINGS

OF

OLD NEW ENGLAND DAYS

Designed and Hooked
at
TURNER VILLAGE, MAINE

Distributed by
George Nicols AND Co., 295 Fifth Ave., New York, N.Y.

The following eight pages are excerpts from a promotional brochure from the Priscilla Turner Rug Guild

Plate I

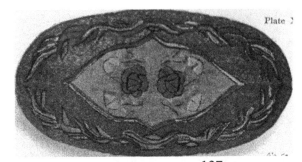

Plate 2

Rug Maker Trainees. Priscilla Turner rugs are the highest quality custom rugs in America. If you are willing to work, can follow directions and have a high school diploma, we offer competitive wages and benefits. Apply in person at Cardinal Enterprises.

Lewiston Journal
March 13, 1987

Human hands can make no finer!

Priscilla Turner rugs, made right in our neighboring town of Turner, represent brilliant achievement in hooked rug styling and hand craftsmanship. Each creation a jewel of pattern beauty, period appeal, color harmony. Deep all-wool pile... styled for contemporary and 18th century rooms as well as for traditional colonial interiors.

Lewiston Daily Sun
March 4, 1948

WHEN, in the latter part of the 18th century, the New England housewife finished her regular household tasks, she usually turned to the various hand crafts and made thrifty use of her odd moments.

Sometimes she busied herself with fancy needlework and often she found delight in fashioning bits of cloth into serviceable mats or rugs.

And so, on winter nights from dusk until bedtime—about eight-thirty—she worked industriously by the light of tallow candles, planning and constructing new and lovely furnishings for the home.

Those were her happiest hours—a time for dreaming as well as for working—with the crackle of the open fire, the purr of the house cat, the hum of the tea kettle to furnish music for her dreams.

Of all the beautiful and useful things she made, none were more charming—or more serviceable—than the quaint hand-made mats. For she fashioned them with great care and worked into their designs something of her thoughts, her moods and her dreams.

Those old mats of hers, though often crude in outline and color, were beautiful in their simplicity. And the patterns were original—a true expression of her individual taste and preferences.

There was a lot of satisfaction in turning the scraps from her rag bag into something useful and beautiful, and those lovely hand-made mats furnished pleasing substitutes for the foreign-made carpets, which were priced beyond her means.

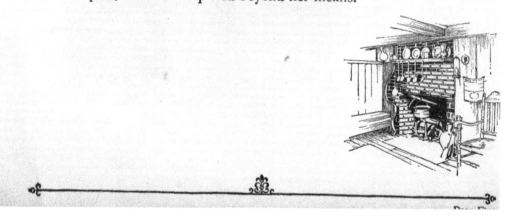

Plate II

That fine old New England handcraft tradition is preserved in Priscilla Turner hooked rugs... each beautiful rug individially created, reflecting conscientious workmanship and care... each luxuriously thick-piled rug made from 100% virgin wool. Women who carefully hook Priscilla Turner rugs are proud of their skill and sign the label attached to the rug. The designs are suited to any decor... add gaily colored accents or richly subdued tones to any room.

Long and Company, the House of Quality Furniture.

Portsmouth Times, July 2, 1955

THERE were many hand-made mats or rugs in Colonial times—braided rugs, knitted rugs, crocheted rugs, rag rugs, scalloped doormats and others. But the most important of all were the "pulled" or hooked rugs.

Hooked rugs were more durable and lent themselves to a wider range of designs than the others.

In making them the worker could include in her pattern—flowers from her garden, birds, ships, animals or . . . anything that pleased her fancy. And the number of colors was limited only by the scraps in her rag bag or by her ability to compound home-made dyes.

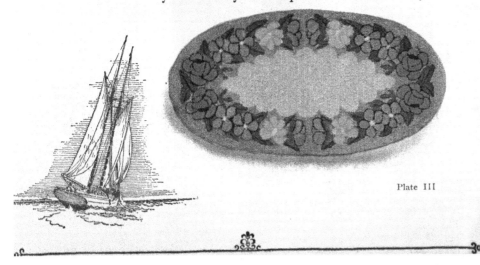

Plate III

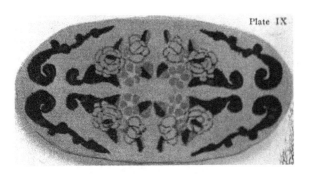

Plate IX

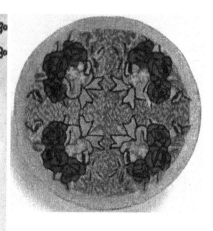

Plate IV

IN the early part of the 19th century, the vogue for hooked rugs grew rapidly throughout New England and in many of the Middle Atlantic states. And, as it grew, a new art was developed—a truly American art.

This art—or craft—flourished for years. But with the invention of the power loom and the advent of machine-made carpets, it suffered a serious setback. Gradually it lost in popularity and soon after the Civil War the art of hooking was forgotten in all but a few communities.

Plate V

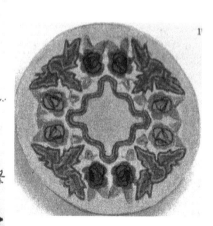

130

My mother, Helen Bryant Ware worked for many years for the Priscilla Turner Rug Guild as a rug hooker. She retired in 1982. I do have a large room size rug she hand-hooked that was purchased on ebay a few years ago. It is currently in storage. I do believe one of her rugs went to the White House many years ago. My husband's mother also worked there as a yarn spinner, putting yarn on spools for the hand-hookers. Her name was Carolyn Libby. I predict you will be overwhelmed by responses from people in the Turner area on this subject. Good luck with the book.
Judy Ware Libby

From left to right:
Helen Bryant Ware ca. 1950's
Large rug hooked by Helen Ware
Helen Bryant Ware ca. 1983

I was only three years old in 1950 when my mother (Helen Bryant Ware) started to work at the Priscilla Turner Rug Shop. Her boss didn't seem to mind that I was often there. On occasion other kids would show up for a day or two, and the kids whose families lived in the village would pop in to see their moms. In my younger years I spent most of my time setting right up on the frame that the canvas was stretched on, while my mother hooked the rugs. I got to know all the ladies, and the four or five men that worked there.

I spent my days gathering up the empty cones that the yarn was wound on and take them back to Carolyn Libby, which she appreciated. The ladies would ask me to get them a spool of yarn that they needed. At first, Carolyn would have to stop the winding of the yarn to help me, but I reached a time when I knew where all the colors were and had the numbers memorized.

I got very attached to one woman, Cindy Newton, who made all the patterns. She had a huge table in a large room in the back of the building. She gave me paper, pencils and rulers of all shapes and sizes and as I watched her design the patterns I would make my own. My mother always told me that was where I got my creativity and sense for putting colors together.

One of the men that worked there was in charge of the backing. Sometimes the pieces were very large and heavy, so he would plop me on top and let me ride along as he delivered it to the hooking room. In the back of the building was an old elevator (a wooden box on cables that you pulled on to raise and lower it between floors). I used to get sent down in that pretty regularly with a machine that needed fixing.

One of my fond memories is the birthday party they had for me when I turned six. I got a pretty yellow frilly apron, just like all the hookers wore, so then I became one of them. I am fortunate to have five rugs my mother made. I remember her saying that it took her whole paycheck that week to pay for one. The Priscilla Turner Rug Shop and the people who worked there will always have a special place in my heart.
Roxanne B. Tremblay

My mother, Wini O'Connor and two of my aunts, Margaret (Peggy) Jordan and Vivian Mancini, worked at the Rug Shop in the early 1960's. On days that the library was opened, we would get off the bus there in the village, stop into Carver's Candy Shop and then we would go to the library and spend some time. (I absolutely loved the library). After that we would go onto the overhead crosswalk and in the second floor door. Mom was working on the third floor on the new tufting machine and most of the floor was wide open so that the tufted rugs could be coated with latex on the bottom. When the floor was not filled, we would push ourselves around the floor on the mechanic crawlers. My aunt would make nets from bent wire and a material like cheesecloth and we would go out to the river and try to catch crawfish, great fun. It wasn't allowed, but my brother went up and down in the materials dumbwaiter. Of course, all our shenanigans were done when the Boss, Mr. Wallace was "not" there. We would take small pieces of yarn and make stick horses. We had them all in different colors.
Anita (O'Connor) Chandler
Monmouth, Maine

Winifred
O'Connor

My grandmother passed two years ago, and this would have been the highlight of her life to talk to someone like you about her and the girls at the rug shop, and anything involved with it. Especially to someone who is, in her words, a fellow hooker.

The little burg of Turner Center was broken into three places-- Turner Village, Turner Center and North Turner, with surrounding towns of Leeds and Greene, where most of these women and men came from. And I would say there are a lot of rugs that were hooked at the Priscilla Turner Rug Guild still in some of the old homesteads and farm houses.

Yes, they were tagged somewhere on the bottom of the rugs with a tag with the ID/Order # and by whom they were hooked. Interesting story, my mom got a Priscilla Turner rug on ebay recently. When it arrived, she discovered that it had been made in the 1950's by her own mother (my grandmother)!

When I was a kid, I spent lots of time in the factory, sometimes making myself useful, sometimes getting up to some mischief or other. I had a lot of "aunts" until I was ten or twelve years old. They'd call up with some yarn that they needed, and I'd ride the dumbwaiter to the third floor to get it. I was a bit of a go-fer for my aunts. Each floor had a bell ring code and there was an inter-phone set up between the floors.

The second floor was mostly the hooking floor. My grandmother had a corner that overlooked the Nesingitt River so she could watch me when I went fishing, as would the rest of my aunts. "Watch Kirk, he's on the river!!" Believe me, I had a short leash. I was the shop hellion, as I was told in later years! I'd watch my grandmother run those Cardinal hand-hooking machines for hours while doing my homework. Sometimes three or four women would work on one together, and after the weight of the yarn, the frame would have to be dogged up to tighten up the rug. I'd help so they didn't have to call Gus or Ray from the machine shop. I remember hearing, "Kirk, sweetie, would you tuft for me?" and I'd take a thin flexible hook and pull lapped yarn and cut it off. That's the best I can explain it-- but after being shown what to do, I knew it meant I could climb under the frame and play in the dust.

All those years of watching those women work those machines, and the machines were old and heavy as hell, but there they were, bent over the tables, pushing and pulling them. Watching their work ethic, they never took vacation or days off. They were just strong willed, and then would go home and cook dinners and wash clothes and bake biscuits and pies. I often reached for my grandmother's hands and held them and asked if they hurt as she grew older. All the bumps, tendon damage, arthritis, and swelling, and she would just smile and set out some aspirin at the table for the next day, and say with a smile, "It's going to be a rough morning. I'll finish a rug and start another." She had "popeye" arms and hands-- all the ladies did-- and if one of them grabbed hold of you, you would know.

Did you know one of the rugs went to the White House? Gram worked on it. I was there the day the paper came to take pictures! I believe it went to the Oval Office. I remember there were two or three ladies working on the Great Seal and it had to be just so and handled with care. Gram got a certificate from the President or someone, and she took great pride in that. Until another one was started-- each one was surely done with pride and care, no matter who it was for-- this I do know.

The first floor had the Patent Room, offices, and shipping and receiving. There was a small showroom and on the river side of course, the machine shop-- which to me was the place of dark surprise and mystery. It was also the dumbwaiter's final stop and the place where my grandfather and his best friend Ray built, fabricated, and every-thing else they had to do to keep the place running. That's also where the only five-cent Coke machine was, and in those days a Coke was a kid's dream-- that and a two-pack of Chicklets.

I spent many weekends helping out in shipping and receiving unloading trailers full of yarn and loading rugs, never a full truck-- usually fifteen or twenty rugs-- but it was quality over quantity.

The Patent Room-- this place was a trip. I'd watch Gus and another man draw and put patterns down on brown paper with a hanging tattoo-type machine, and then roll it and tube it until needed. Then they'd stretch the backing, lay the brown paper over it, ink paint the drawing holes and "bingo!" a rug was started. Some ladies would come look at it and figure out colors and go over it, and before you knew it, they would start hooking.
Kirk Henson
Ayer, MA

NOVELTY
EMBROIDERY AND
Rug Machine,

Patented March 4th 1884.

We are now prepared to furnish this useful practical and convenient device to all those who wish to ornament their homes with beautiful and artistically designed Rugs, of any desired Size or Pattern.

With the Novelty Rug Machine, Rugs of most exquisite design and finish are easily and rapidly made with it, you can make the most beautiful Rug in a few hours that would require weeks of labor with a hook, and the Machine makes the loops more even than usually done by hand.

Mittens, Hoods, Tidies, Lap Robes, Door Mats, etc., can also be made with it.

Works equally well with either Yarn or Rags. With the aid of this Machine any lady can produce at a very moderate outlay of time and money Rugs equal in appearance and durability to imported hand-made Turkish Rugs costing from $10.00 to $100.00.

We send the Machine to any address on receipt of $1.00 with full printed directions for use together with patterns to commence with.

We want Agents in every City and Town where we now have none at work. It is the best article ever invented for Ladies or Gentlemen to sell at Fairs, in Stores, or Canvassing and many are now coining money with it. Write at once for our terms and secure your territory.

Address,

THE HUDSON MANUFACTURING CO.,

265 SIXTH AVENUE, N. Y

I went to work in November, 1960 at the Priscilla Turner Rug Shop, intending to work until after Christmas, but ended up working there for 30 years. I worked on the first floor, cutting the backing for the size of the rugs being made, finishing and hemming after the rug was finished. It was sometimes quite a job with the big rugs. They had to have more people to help turn and move the rug around while hooking. Small ones were such that one person could do it.

When we moved to Center St. in Auburn, Maine, I became the rug hooker. I made rugs for Alan Lundan, Betty White, Captain Kangaroo, resorts in Rockland, Maine, plus many more. Sometimes samples were made for the customer as they would send in articles to match like door knobs, drapery material, dinner plates, and many other items they wanted the rug to match. Sometimes there were flowers the size of a dime with five or six different colors.

The machines weighed about 12 pounds so after an 8-hour day you were ready to go home, as you knew you had worked a full day.

You were allowed to bring your children to work. There was one boy who was with us quite a lot. His name was Patrick Dempsey, he was a cute little boy like he is now a handsome man. Who would ever think that a little boy playing with trucks and yarn balls would ever be this famous?

I moved wherever they moved, and ended up working there for over 30 years. It was hard work, especially on your back, but we had good times too.

Virginia Gross, Rug Hooker
Turner, Maine

Priscilla Turner Rug 5'10"x4'
Photo courtesy of Judy Raymond

Priscilla Turner Rug   Artichoke Hearts 6'x9'
Hooked by Audrey Hobbs-Dean Custom-made Registry #8610-81
Courtesy of Dianne Maillet, Athens, TN

Magazine ad October 1946

If you appreciate the finest in traditional American handcraft... if you indulge yourself in exquisite touches of decorative refinement in your home... Priscilla Turner hooked rugs are created to give your home the mark of your individual personality.

When you see these beautiful rugs... when you feel them--- by touch or underfoot--- you sense immediately the discerning taste fulfilled in their designs and colors... the pride of the conscientious craftsman in making a product that genuinely joins quality to beauty.

Knowing this... proud of the old New England tradition they are perpetuating... proud too of their skill... each maker of a Priscilla Turner hooked rug personally signs the label attached to your rug.

Always look for the label which guarantees you the finest virgin wool, spun and scoured in American Mills, clean as the fibers in a baby's garment.

The Telegraph, Nashua, NH
March 4, 1952

(opposite page)
Needlecraft Magazine September 1931

Popular Priscilla Rug Patterns At New Low Prices

No. 28-1-8. Size, 26 x 41 inches. Stamped on tan burlap, $1.00
The Old Homestead—white house under the green elms

We supply rug yarns in black and colors at 35 cents a skein

No. 27-7-8. (above) Chair-seat or cushion top. Size, 15 inch. Stamped on tan burlap, 35 cents

No. 27-7-9. (at left) Chair-seat or cushion top. Size, 15 inch. Stamped on tan burlap, 35 cents

171 N. Rug frame of wood 24 x 36 inches 85 cents

25N. Rug Hook 25 cents

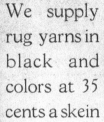

No. 26-8-1. Size, 29 x 57 inches. Stamped on tan burlap, $1.00

No. 26-1-15. Size, 34 x 56 inches. Stamped on tan burlap, $1.00. Snow scene, green firs, gray-blue icy brook, gorgeous sun and sunset sky

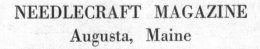

No. 25-8-1. Size, 28 x 38 inches. Stamped on tan burlap, 75 cents

We have selected here those patterns which most nearly resemble the popular patterns of olden times and which now bring the most fabulous prices in antique shops. Any one of these patterns is well worth your time in making it. Order by number and send your orders to

NEEDLECRAFT MAGAZINE
Augusta, Maine

No. 27-5-35. Size, 20 x 27 inches. Stamped on tan burlap, 50 cents

These four rugs were featured in a Priscilla Turner catalog ca. 1930's

139

Solitude 38.5" W x 21.5" H   (2012)
Adapted from a photograph that I took of the view from our window on a family trip to the Faroe Islands.

Rug hooking is a wonderful medium for expressing your artistic vision: it is simple to learn, it isn't expensive to do, it is fun and relaxing, and you can do it in whatever little bits of free time you have. These are all very important to me as a mother of young children. As with any art, though, the hardest part is often just getting started.

The most important step to making a successful rug is having a clear vision in your mind before you begin. My most important piece of advice for any artist is to always carry a camera, and to use it! The majority of my ideas are taken from snapshots of candid life moments, striking landscapes or memorable colour combinations in nature. I keep a box of photos that I have taken just so that I always have lots of ideas to mix and match into new compositions. It doesn't matter whether your picture is taken with the camera on your phone or with a fancy lens so long as you have something to help you remember your idea.

The second most important thing is to know what you like, and to do that rather than what you might think other people are expecting to see. I love unexpected colours and colour combinations wherever I see them and it often only takes a few seconds to pull over, roll down the car window and snap a picture of them. I love the colours of autumn at home in Ontario, summer all around the North Atlantic, and especially the fantastic combinations that surprise you all over Iceland.

Krisuvik 12" W x 12" H   (2009)
At a corner in the road along the southwest shore of Iceland, there is a lonely little church set on a small knoll. There is nothing else around but windswept rock, hardy grass and moody sky. Adapted from my own photograph.

Moss-Covered Lava Rocks, Iceland
12.5" W x 16" H   (2009)
The roads through the Reykjanes Peninsula in southeast Iceland pass through great fields of old, broken lava.
The lava rocks are often covered in thick blankets of moss that can take on quite surprising colours. Adapted
from my own photograph.

Iceland Mosaic
59" W x 28.5" H   (2008)
On the road from Hveragerdi to Selfoss in Iceland, you pass a church sitting on a small bluff overlooking the farms and horse stables. This is my own design based on different aspects of several of my own photographs.

Perhaps the most enlightening lesson I have learned as a rug hooker is the importance of understanding the basics of light, colour and perspective. I had cross-stitched kits for many years before I picked up my first hook but I discovered very quickly that that wasn't the same as making original designs. I had never tried to draw and I had even convinced myself that I couldn't. Rug hooking opened my eyes not just to the possibilities of original designs but also to the wider world of art. I've had a lot of fun visiting galleries and museums and studying the painters I really enjoy to see firsthand what it was that they did with their colours that caught my eye.

The Tree Climber 19" W x 15" H   (2011)
Adapted from a photograph that my husband took of our young daughter climbing a tree to get a better view of the world around her.

Colours of Mud at Hverir, Iceland
12.5" W x 12.5" H   (2012)
Adapted from a photograph that I took of the fascinating and unique colours found within the steaming mud pools of Iceland.

This and learning to draw helped me to better understand how I can capture an idea in a rug and increased my versatility as an artist.

I hook exclusively with yarn primarily because of the higher resolution it enables than the larger wool cuts. This means that I can incorporate more detail into an area and, since there isn't a lot of time each day in my young family for hooking, that means I can make smaller designs that I can carry with me wherever in the house I happen to get a chance to sit. *Krisuvik* is only a 12 inch square, and the six small sections of *Solitude* are each about the size of a postcard! For the same reason, I work almost exclusively with pre-dyed wools since it eliminates any extra preparation time to either dye my wool or cut my strips. The unintended side benefit of this approach is that I have visited a lot of wool stores on my travels and received a lot of gifts from thoughtful family and friends so that I have now built up a wonderful 'palette' of my favourite colours. Sometimes I look through my palette and an idea begins by deciding that I just really want to use a particular colour.

I think the most satisfying part of rug hooking is relaxing while I mix colours into an enjoyable project in whatever manner takes my fancy at the time. Getting there takes planning, though, and oftentimes a good deal of faith to just see the rug through to the end. Any rug in the beginning looks to me like it will never become what I imagine for it!

Hesturinn
29" W x 25" H   (2010)
Icelandic for "horse." This piece is adapted from a photograph that I took of a horse standing in the sunny fields above the Gulfoss waterfall in Iceland. The mountains of the interior were silhouetted in this eye-catching deep blue by a passing storm.

Girl with a Yellow Bucket 17" W x 27" H   (2010)
My daughter loves investigating beaches, like this one at Lac Simon, Quebec. I wanted to capture the essence of toddlerhood through the bright colours and the eager excitement of her body language. Adapted from my own photograph.

View from Captain Cook's Monument 12.5" W x 15" H   (2010)
This piece was adapted from a photograph that I took of the Bay of Islands from the top of Captain Cook's monument in Corner Brook, Newfoundland, Canada.

The first question I address when designing a project is the basic composition. This step can just be cropping and magnifying if you are fortunate enough to be working from a well-composed photograph. Otherwise, the rule of thirds is a great guide for assembling your focal point, background and foreground elements into an interesting landscape or scene. *Solitude* is an example of both of these approaches at the same time. It was inspired by an actual view through a holiday cottage window but it had to be adapted by moving the house to conform to the rule of thirds.

The next question for me is the size. While there is no limit to how big you can make a piece, there is a minimum size that is determined by your resolution. The piece can't be any smaller than is required to allow you to make the smallest necessary detail in the project. Given that I prefer to work with smaller pieces, this consideration is usually my starting point. For example, when I decided that I wanted to detail the individual fingers on the girl in *Tree Climber* and the eye of the bird in *Atlantic Mascot*, those decisions determined the size of the rest of those figures, and of the rest of both compositions.

I draw exact guidelines on my rug warp for anything in the composition that has to be hooked precisely and credibly, which is usually the focal point. In realistic artwork, this means carefully observing proportions, perspective and shading. A puffin is instantly recognizable but its iconic sad expression can easily be lost if it is overdone. A human figure is immeasurably enhanced by even the most basic shading. The perspective on a building can be deliberately distorted and still look very pleasing, so long as it is done consistently throughout.

Any line that isn't consistent with your plan will be instantly and unpleasantly noticeable. I always hook these elements of the rug first, and as many times as necessary, because I know that until these elements work the way I imagine them, I won't be able to move on to the rest of the rug.

As careful as I am with the focal point, I am much more relaxed about mapping out the foreground and the background. It is a matter of personal choice, but I like to avoid distractions from my focal points in my compositions. The actual background behind the puffin that inspired *Atlantic Mascot* was very complex and interesting in its own right. The overall effect was so busy that the puffin was almost lost. Instead, I mimicked the effect of the same background taken out of focus in other photos. Similarly in *Girl with a Yellow Bucket*, the background is significantly simplified relative to the detail of the girl and the wet sand she is walking on to avoid distraction.

I am also very relaxed about mapping out abstract pieces. These pieces, like *Colours of Mud in Hverir, Iceland*, are all about colour selection and while I did have a photo I had taken of the mud pool to guide me, I only mapped out the general proportions of the swirl in the mud before beginning.

Choice of colours and materials can also enliven a piece. The flat background blues in *Solitude* establish the whole mood of the piece, and I had to re-do it a couple of times to get it right! The blues had to be just right in order to establish the contrast I was trying to capture between the dark sky after an Atlantic gale compared to the brilliant white of the breaking waves, the green of the seaside pastureland and the striking red of the house next door. One of my other favourite techniques is to use novelty yarns to enliven what would otherwise be a monotonous section of foreground or background. The water in *Solitude* contains touches of sparkly ribbon that really helped to convey the motion of the water. The foregrounds in *Krisuvik* and *Atlantic Mascot* capture the sense of dry grass moving in the wind by using a riot of polyester strands. The problem with relying on pre-dyed novelty yarns is that the colour selection is obviously quite limited relative to basic yarn, but when the colours are right, they are an excellent resource!

The final consideration when planning a piece is how it will be finished, and specifically whether it will be framed. Just like a painting, framing can sometimes finish a piece. I found in general that abstract pieces like *Colours of Mud in Hverir, Iceland* needed something to put a boundary around the composition. A frame can even be as much a part of the composition as the rug itself if you use 'found' frames or interesting wood to make them. *Solitude* is framed in an antique window frame. Just remember when laying out a piece intended to fit into an existing frame that your piece will expand as you work so remember to keep checking that it is still fitting as it should. *Solitude* is composed of seven independent pieces mounted in the panes of the window so it had to be checked frequently to ensure that all the horizon lines, roof lines, windows and siding were all still lining up. A far easier approach was used for *Colours of Mud in Hverir, Iceland* and *Atlantic Mascot*, which both used custom frames made out of driftwood so no pre-planning was required in the actual hooking.

Have Fun!

With all the planning done, all that remains for you to do is to enjoy hooking your project!

Karen Miller has been designing and hooking her own rugs at Marzipan Road since 2008.

You can visit her at www.marzipanroad.com.

Atlantic Mascot 21" W x 21" H   (2012)
A puffin sits on a grassy hill, guarding its burrow.
Based on a photograph that I took from a recent
trip to Iceland.

PROJECTS

I use many different methods for creating shading in my hooked rugs; dip-dyeing, successive dyeing, overdyeing, blending colors with handspun yarn, and plying different colors of handspun. In this chapter you will find lots of small practice projects, so you can try the different techniques that you have read about in this book.

Pam's Family 24"x18"
Designed and hooked by Kay LeFevre

Dip-dyed hibiscus

I hooked this Hibiscus project to demonstrate the many ways you can do shading. Above left you see one that I hooked using a dip-dyed grey and white yarn. I then overdyed that same yarn in Autumn dye to hook the Hibiscus lower left.

Overdyed dip-dyed hibiscus

Progressive dyed hibiscus

This time I used progressive dyeing to create three shades of grey and white for the Hibiscus above left. Then I overdyed those yarns in Autumn dye to hook the Hibiscus lower left.

Overdyed progressive dyed hibiscus

Handspun blended hibiscus

The Hibiscus above left was hooked with handspun blended Jacob wool. The Hibiscus lower left was hooked with the same yarn, overdyed with Autumn.

I always find it easier to practice shading with shades of grey, but you can always overdye your grey samples, whether they are handspun blended yarns, dip-dyed yarns or yarns that were dyed progressively.

Use the Hibiscus pattern on page 151 to practice shading techniques.

Overdyed blended hibiscus

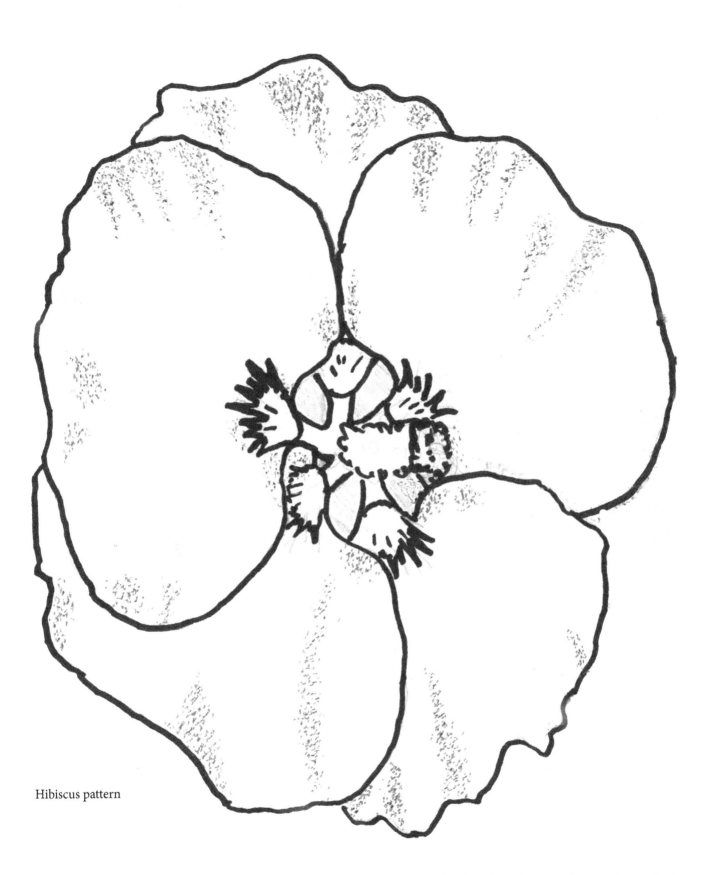

Hibiscus pattern

Use this Hibiscus pattern to practice dip-dyeing, progressive dyeing, blending handspun colors and overdyeing to practice the many methods to create shading. You will use these methods individually and in combination to create realistic shading in your future rug designs.

Alpaca mat 6"x6.75"
Designed and hooked by Judy Taylor

The Alpaca design is great for practicing dip-dyeing (the mane all around the face was hooked with dip dyed yarn) and progressive dyeing (the shading inside the face). Then try overdyeing your yarn to create a different colored alpaca.

Alpaca pattern

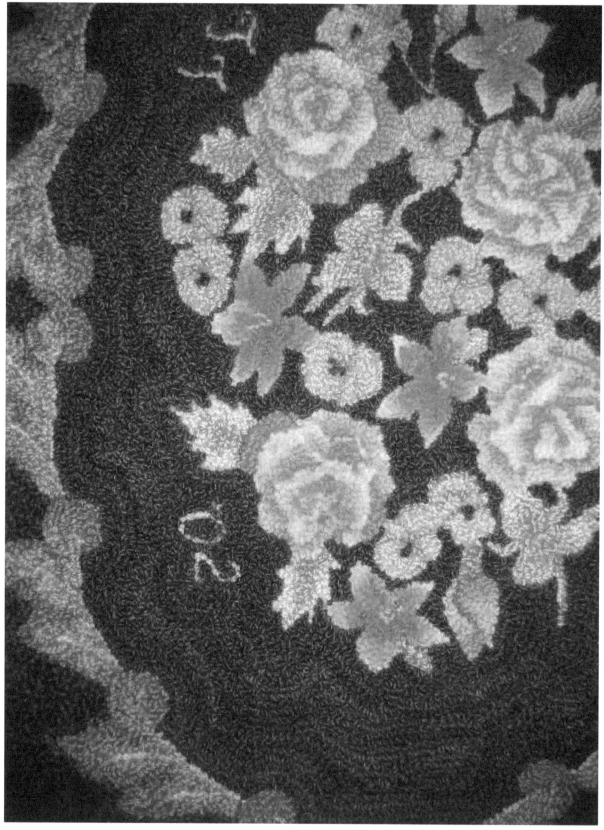

Close up of Antique Flower Rug
Designed and hooked by Judy Taylor

The patterns for the flowers and scrolls in this design are included in the following pages. You can combine some or all of these features in your own practice project.

HOOKING THE ROSE

The key to making a rose look like a rose is to create a contrast between the highlight at the outside of the petal and the lowlight or the shadow at the base of the petal beneath it. Beginning with the darker end of the strand (1) hook each petal from the inside to the outside, always hooking in the same direction. I don't necessarily start with the very darkest end of the strand. That way, they don't all fade out at the same rate.

Rose pattern
1- dip-dyed pink
2- dip-dyed spring green

Don't worry if while you are hooking the rose it doesn't look like a rose. You really need to hook the whole thing, and cut off all the ends, and look at it from a distance. What seems like abstract blobs of color up close may surprise you when you see it from afar. Then you can decide if you need to add more highlight or lowlight to make the design clear.

To hook the leaves, begin in the center of the leaf, hooking with the darkest end of the spring green yarn (2). Keep radiating out from the inside of the leaf to the outside, dark to light.

HOOKING THE CLEMATIS

Beginning in the center of the clematis, hook the stamens, using only the yellow end of the yellow-purple strands (6). Then hook the folds in the petals (5). Next hook each petal from the inside out, starting with the darkest end of the strawberry dip-dyed yarn (4). Try to create a contrast between petals by hooking a slightly darker edge on the petals toward the back, meeting up with a lighter edge on the petals in the foreground.

To hook the leaves, beginning at the outside end of the spine, hook with the lightest end of the kiwi (7). Then turn the corner so the darker part of the dip-dyed kiwi fills the outside of the petal.

Clematis pattern
3- solid dark blue
4- dip-dyed strawberry
5- solid red
6- yellow yarn, dip-dyed purple
7- dip-dyed kiwi

155

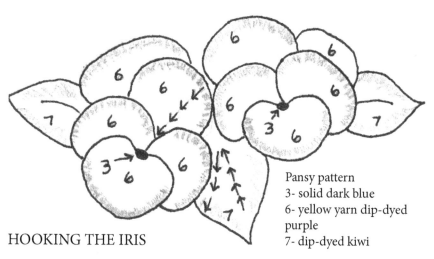

Pansy pattern
3- solid dark blue
6- yellow yarn dip-dyed purple
7- dip-dyed kiwi

HOOKING THE PANSY

Beginning at the outside of the pansy this time, and starting with the purple end of the yellow-purple strand (6) hook toward the center dot (3). You really only want a little purple on the outside edge of each petal. You want the color to change to yellow by the time you reach the bottom of each petal so it will contrast with the outside edge of the petal in front of it.

HOOKING THE IRIS

First hook the stamens, using the yellow part of the yellow-purple strands (6). Then hook each petal, starting in the center and hooking outwards using the purple yarn (8). Try to create contrast between the front center petal and the two lower side petals by hooking more dark in the base of the side leaves, meeting up with some of the lighter purple on the sides of the center petal.

To hook the leaves, start at the upper end of the top of the leaf with the darker end of the kiwi (7). Then turn around and hook up the bottom of the leaf with the lighter end of the kiwi.

Iris pattern
6- yellow yarn dip-dyed purple
7- dip-dyed kiwi
8- dip-dyed purple

HOOKING THE SCROLLS

The scrolls need a "base" to distinguish them from the background color, so I used the strawberry (4). Starting at the bottom of the scroll, with the darkest end, I just hooked a line up to the curley-cue.

Then, just above the strawberry line, hook the vein of the scroll, using spring green (2). Starting with the darkest end of the yarn, hook the veins so they get lighter as they radiate out.

Starting at the bottom of the scroll, begin hooking up from the veins with the evergreen-rose color (9). Start with the green end at the bottom, so that the tips of the scroll will be rose colored.

You may need to use some extra rose in the curley-cue so that you create a contrast between it and the bottom of the next scroll.

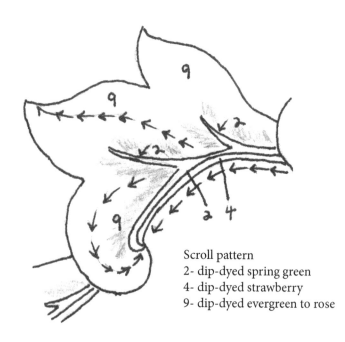

Scroll pattern
2- dip-dyed spring green
4- dip-dyed strawberry
9- dip-dyed evergreen to rose

Lovebirds 21.5"x30"
Designed and hooked by Judy Taylor

Lovebirds pattern detail #1

Use these templates to create your own version of Lovebirds. With primitive designs like these, you may find it helpful to transfer these to paper as you see them here, but when you want to draw the other half of the pattern, try freehanding the other side, as opposed to flipping the pattern. This way you will create the subtle variation and unevenness that makes primitive rugs unique.

Lovebirds pattern detail #2

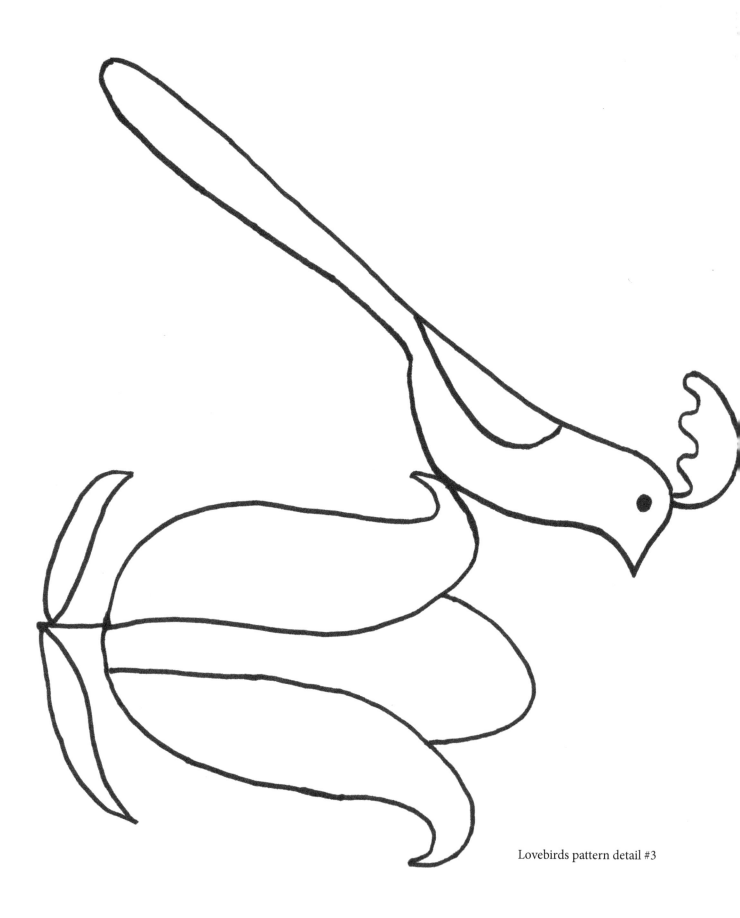

Lovebirds pattern detail #3

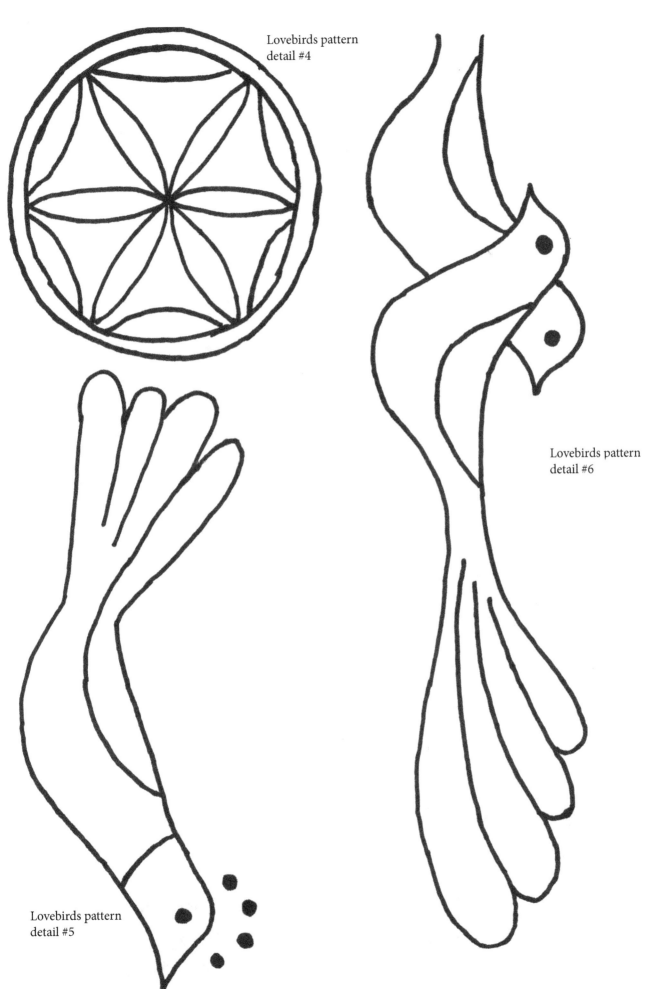

Lovebirds pattern
detail #4

Lovebirds pattern
detail #6

Lovebirds pattern
detail #5

161

Left: Lovebirds pattern
detail #7

Right: Counting Sheep
pattern detail

Brementown 23.5"x31"
Designed and hooked by Judy Taylor

Brementown pattern detail #1

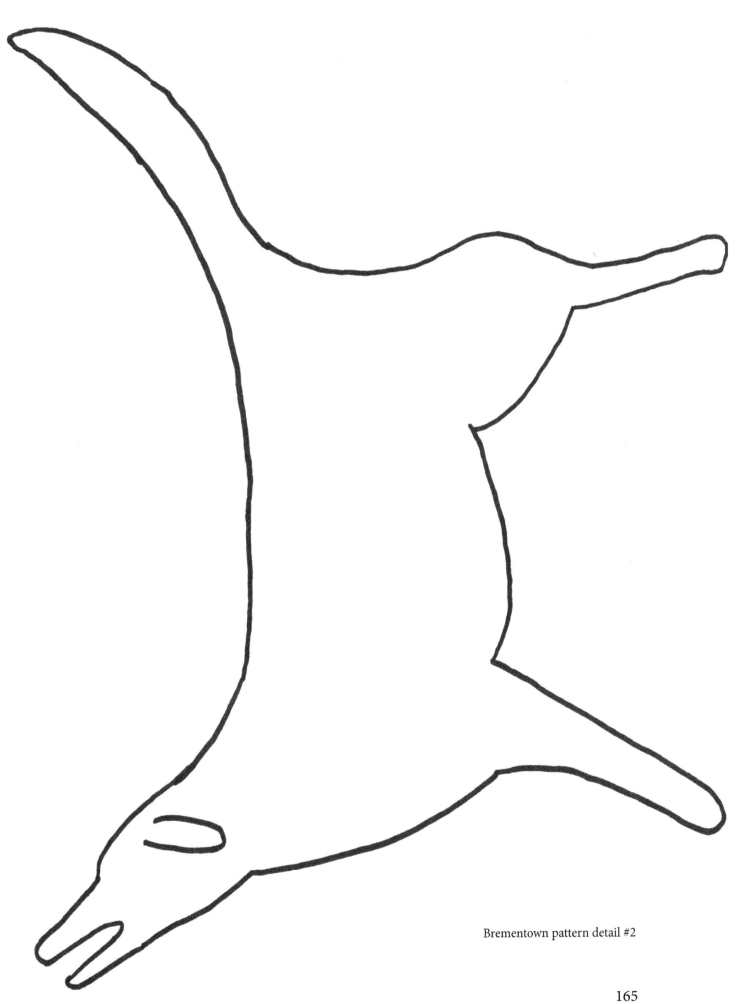

Brementown pattern detail #2

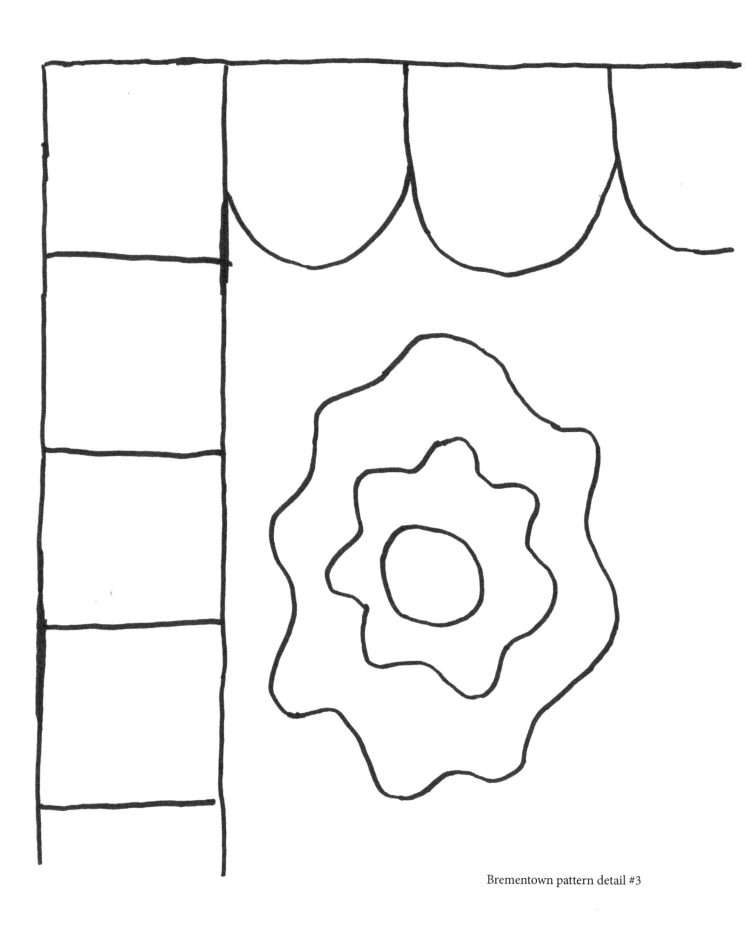

Brementown pattern detail #3

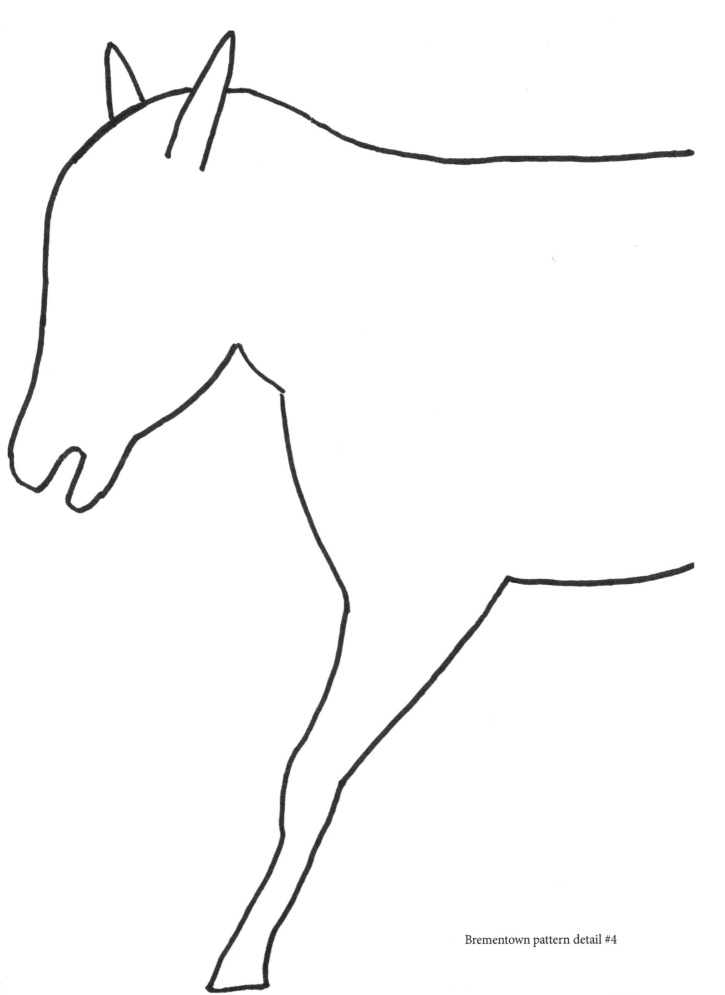

Brementown pattern detail #4

Brementown pattern detail #5

Turkish Delight 20.5"x31"
Designed and hooked by Judy Taylor

Magic Carpet 35"x26"
Designed and hooked by Judy Taylor

170

Magic Carpet pattern detail #1

Magic Carpet pattern detail #2

Use these oriental design templates to create your own designs. If you use them to scale as provided here, they will give you a chance to practice creating fine detail. However, you can always enlarge the templates to make the designs larger and easier to hook.

Turkish Delight pattern detail #1

Turkish Delight pattern detail #2

Turkish Delight pattern detail #3

Magic Carpet pattern detail #3

Magic Carpet pattern detail #4

Oriental pattern detail #1

Oriental pattern detail #2

Oriental pattern detail #3

Oriental pattern detail #4

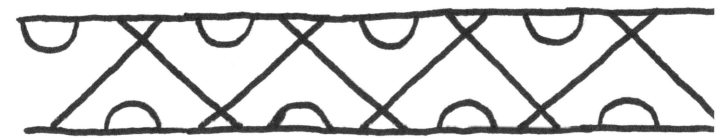

Oriental pattern detail #5

Oriental pattern detail #6

Magic Carpet pattern detail #5

Magic Carpet pattern detail #6

Oriental pattern detail #7

Oriental pattern detail #8

Oriental pattern detail #9

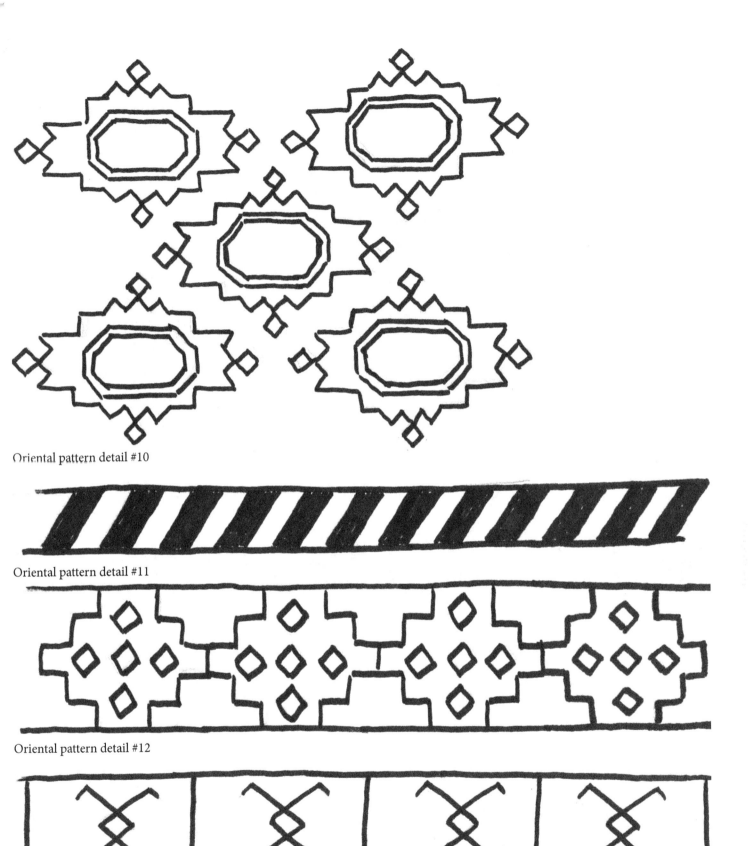

Oriental pattern detail #10

Oriental pattern detail #11

Oriental pattern detail #12

Oriental pattern detail #13

Featured Artist
Sharon Johnston
Calgary, Alberta

Memorial Library, Calgary 1912 16"x24"
Designed and hooked by Sharon Johnston, from an old postcard. The detail and shading were the hardest part of this building to do. This commissioned piece was for the building's 100th anniversary.

I was first introduced to rug hooking filling a space in a beginner's class, but it did not appeal to me, way too many rules. Some photos in a book caught my eye and on reading more on the subject decided to give it another try. Having read that you could hook with almost anything, and having bags of leftover fabrics, I started hooking with them. We were selling our house and I thought it would be easier to move a rug than all those fabric strips I had kept. Since then I have been hooked, my stash has grown even larger!

Through my art I came to rug hooking, having taken up drawing, painting and collage. From an early age I have been involved with textiles; sewing, batik, painting on fabric, and anything involving fabrics and yarns. Since I started rug hooking textiles have become my medium and palette of colours, and I keep experimenting with the medium, trying new and different fibers. I also like the fact that hooking is a traditional craft that is still alive and growing.

I have always incorporated yarn in my fabric hookings. Lately I have been hooking only with only yarn to use up my ever growing stash. The beauty of yarn is the wonderful supply of colours, thickness, and textures that can be used in so many ways. Yarn doesn't require cutting, which is a big time saver and can be as long as you want, working well on most backing material. The loops can be pulled high, low, twisted and sculptured.

The beauty of hooking is that you need only learn one stitch, leaving lots of room for creativity. One need not get caught up in a whole lot of rules either. There is not really a need for much in the way of tools. Make your own as the early settlers did. I have homemade frames, some are old picture frames adapted for hooking, steel crochet hooks that my husband makes handles for, scissors, fabric and yarns I have collected, and a head full of ideas. It is amazing what we can create with these simple everyday things and enjoy the process and the people we meet through this fiber art community. Hooking is a traditional craft that is alive today and growing with new creative ideas.

Hooking with yarn is fun and easy, as you don't need to cut fabric into strips and can hook any length you want without stopping and starting with a new strip. I also like hooking the yarns at different heights, hooking from the reverse side or using embroidery stitches, or clipping the yarn for even more textures. Like most hooking, the direction and way you hook (twisting, straight loops and height) makes a difference in the look you achieve. Mixing yarn with other materials gives me even greater variations in my work.

Organic 25" diameter
Designed and hooked by Sharon Johnston
2011 Calgary Stampede Arts & Crafts 1st in class and 2nd in section

This was my first attempt at an all wool yarn rug. The idea came from a photo I took of an end of an old log as the textures and colours drew me into it. There is a fair amount of pixillation with the yarn to create the different colours and have them blend.

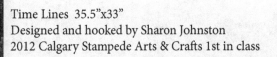

Time Lines 35.5"x33"
Designed and hooked by Sharon Johnston
2012 Calgary Stampede Arts & Crafts 1st in class

I had so enjoyed hooking the log end, I have started working on a series of these rugs. In Time Lines, I wanted to explore the bark texture, and the circles in the wood. This piece was also designed from my photo of where a large branch had been cut off and the double circles were an unusual feature. Some see a face in it. The cut area is hooked slightly lower with a raised scar around it, and then bark at mid-height.

I start with a rough sketch of my idea and decide on size and shape and think about the colours I will use. Think dark/light and warm/cool, when color planning. Next, check to see if you have enough yarn on hand for the project. Of course, you can adapt changes once you are hooking if you run out.

Use a backing fabric that you are comfortable with. I prefer linen or rug warp. Once you have cut your piece on straight grain allowing extra for finishing, I like to sew around the edge to prevent fraying, even running a line of fabric glue just inside the sewing as an extra caution.

Taking shape and dimensions into account, make an outline all around the edge of the design with a permanent felt pen. I then like to divide this in thirds and make a light pencil line and also mark the centre of the design area.

If you are using a photo or sketch, simplify to the most necessary to convey your idea. Find the darkest and lightest areas and outline them, then the other colour values you will need to use. Once you have this you can draw your design and enlarge it to the rug size. If you are using several items in your rug you may want to make separate patterns of each and enlarge to size and cut them out so they can be placed or moved around once you are ready to transfer pattern or design to backing. If you want, you can draw directly onto the backing first with pencil and then outline your design with a permanent pen.

Ladies of the Night 34"x23"
Designed and hooked by Sharon Johnston
Hooked on linen using assorted fabrics, yarn, leather, lace, ribbon and assorted embellishments. The design idea came from Robert Service's poem "The Harpy," the rug is my tribute to these pioneer women. It won second place in the 2011 Western Class at the Calgary Stampede.

Stretch your designed piece on a frame and just start hooking, laying the yarn over the hook to prevent separation of fibers. I like to work all over the design first placing in my dark areas and then light ones and gradually filling in the other colours and values from centre out toward edges. You can hook at different heights, with thick and thinner yarns, and in any direction or randomly. Yarns can be mixed, twisting two or more thinner ones together, or pixillated by pulling loops up between other coloured loops. This method is useful for blending two colors and for shading.

There are so many textured and coloured yarns available, it is seldom necessary to dye them, and the challenge is to make what you have work. Repeated shapes in different sizes and slightly different colours and values helps keep the design balanced and harmonious. A surprise element can also add interest.

Don't be afraid to be creative, it is important to make it your own and to enjoy doing it. Happy hooking!

(opposite page)
Boom Town 24"x25"
Designed by Sharon Johnston in collaboration with John Vickers, graphic artist
2012 Calgary Stampede Arts & Crafts 1st in class and 1st in section

Each year the Stampede has a class about Alberta and the western heritage. 2012 was the 100th anniversary of the Stampede. Since the first boom was during this period, I wanted to tell it's story but also something about the city. My son-in-law helped with the background, emphasizing main features about the city and important industry, keeping it simple. I added some of the buildings built then and things that were important to that boom. I also made suggestion as to what was to fuel future booms. This small rug was designed and hooked in about a month.

BASIC RUG HOOKING INSTRUCTIONS

Here you will find an abbreviated set of instructions for basic rug hooking. For a more detailed introduction to the craft, including instructions for hooking with fabric strips, check out *Joy of Hooking (With Yarn!)*.

You may have noticed that many of the guest artists in this book use a punch hook. I don't include instructions for punch hooking, because firstly, I don't hook in that style, so I wouldn't make a very good teacher! Try books by Amy Oxford for some really great instruction and inspiration. I feel strongly, and I recommend to all my students, that you should try both methods, to see which one works best for you. Once you settle on the method that you are comfortable with, all the rest of the creative stuff in this book works just as well with punching as with hooking in the traditional style.

To begin hooking with yarn: Sit with your knees comfortably apart (about 9") with the backing across your lap (design side up). Tuck the backing snugly under the outside of your thighs, so that you can pull the backing somewhat taut across your lap. Your lap becomes your "frame" (you can also use frames that are specially designed for Nantucket rug hooking at www.littlehouserugs.com).

Hold the hook in your right hand (if you are right-handed) and have the ball of yarn that you are working with between your legs under the backing. Hold the yarn with your left hand under the backing. Your left hand should go underneath on the inside of the backing, rather than trying to reach around the outside to hold your yarn. If you are starting with a small kit, you might be able to get away with reaching around the outside (although to me it seems uncomfortable), but when you get to hooking larger projects like floor rugs, you won't be able to reach around at all. Think of it like you're holding a plate in front of you, with one hand above and one hand underneath.

Push in the hook where you want to begin. For your very first try at rug hooking, I recommend starting with a solid-colored area so you can get the "hang" of it before you attempt to do the detail areas. Later, when you understand the hooking process better, you will always want to begin with the detailed sections, because the pattern lines tend to get obscured when you hook around them. But for your first time hooking, just start in the background area until you get an idea of how far apart to place your loops. (Figure 1)

Push your hook through the backing, from the top, and connect with the yarn below; then pull the end up through the backing, to the top. Leave about a 1" 'tail' of yarn sticking up for now. You will cut this off later, but you need to leave it in place for the time being. Next choose a hole near the tail (usually right next to the tail, or skipping one thread in the backing, depending on how thick the yarn is) and put your hook in again, down through the backing. (Figure 2)

Your left hand can hold up the backing initially, so you have something to push your hook against, until you get your hook through, but then "slide" down the yarn with your left hand for a couple of inches. Notice that I am not letting the yarn flop around underneath, I have it under control in my left hand all the time.

Then, still holding the yarn underneath with your left hand, lift that part of the yarn up, push the hook down from the top, and connect the yarn between your left thumb and fingers onto your hook. (Figure 3)

It really helps if you hold the yarn on the hook with your left hand until you pull the loop through to the top. This keeps the yarn connected to the hook, so you avoid "splitting the yarn." (Figure 4)

Once you have pulled the yarn through to the top, let go with your left hand underneath and feel the slack in the yarn pulling up. (Figure 5 shows the slack pulling up after the hook has been pulled through to the top.)

As soon as you feel with your left hand that you have pulled up all the yarn, stop pulling from above. The reason to give yourself that slack in the yarn is so that you do not pull out the previous loop. (Figure 6 shows the slack pulled snug in the back. Figure 7 shows what the right hand is doing at the same time)

Next, with your left hand, pull the loop on top of the backing (Figure 8) down to the desired height, usually about 1/8 of an inch. In general, the loop should be about as tall as the yarn is wide. If you are making a floor rug--where durability is the goal--short, densely packed loops wear the best. However, if you are making a wall-hanging, you can make your loops a little higher. Practice making all your loops the same height. Notice that if you do not give yourself enough slack in the yarn, you are liable to pull out the previous loop.

Figure 1

183

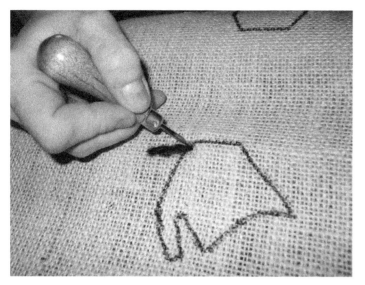

Figure 2

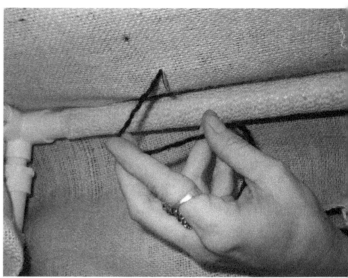

Figure 3

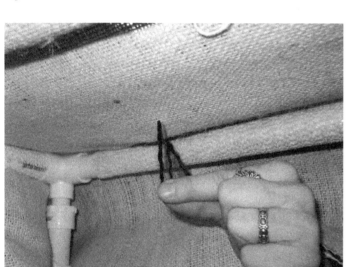

Figure 4

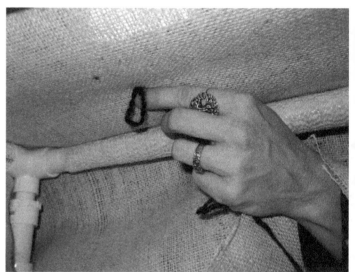

Figure 5

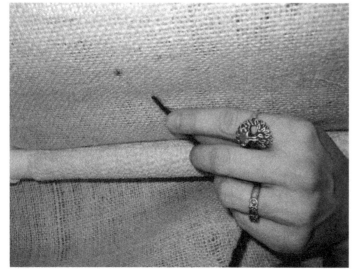

Figure 6

Figure 7

Figure 8

Figure 9

Figure 10

When you come to the end of a section and you want to switch to a different yarn or a different area of the rug, bring up the last loop, just as if you were going to make another loop, but this time cut the yarn on the top and pull the remaining yarn out the back with your left hand. Now you have two tails sticking up, one when you began and one when you finished. These tails need to remain in place until they are surrounded by other loops, at which time you can cut them from above, even with the loops around them. They are held in place by the pressure of the loops around them, and they seem to disappear. (Figure 9)

It may seem precarious to leave the tails like that without tying a knot or anything, but in fact, this is one of the keys to the longevity of these hooked rugs. Sometime during the life of this rug, ten, twenty, fifty years from now, that rug may need to be repaired. Because we do not tie knots, we can always pull out yarn in the damaged areas and re-hook them. The loops in hooked rugs should not pull out with normal wear and tear (walking on them, vacuuming or washing), but occasionally a bit of yarn can get snagged (kitties are often the culprit!), stained or worn, and what is so great about these rugs is that they can always be repaired.

When hooking with yarn, it is helpful to occasionally look at the back. All of the yarn should be pulled tight across the back. Yarn needs room to spread out across the top, so there should be space bewteen the rows. (Figure 10)

Finishing and Hemming

The way that you finish your rug depends on how you plan to use it. For a wall hanging, a simple turned under hem can be sufficient. If you are hemming corners on a rectangular rug, first cut away the corner edge of the backing, so it will not add extra bulk to the corner hem (Figure 11). Then you can fold the extra backing underneath to make a mitred corner which should lie nice and flat (Figures 13 and 14).

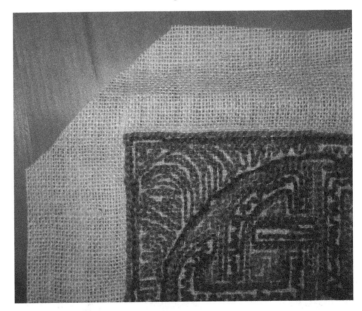

Figure 11

185

Figure 13

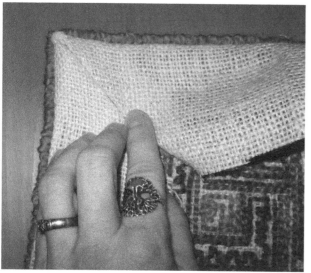

Figure 14

Figure 15

If you are designing a rug for the floor, it is important to bind the edges of the rug before you hem. Begin by trimming awas the extra linen, leaving about 3" beyond the hooked area. Trim the corners away to reduce bulk. (Figure 16)

Figure 16

For this process, purchase cotton cording from the fabric store (3/16" works well). Wrap your backing around the cord, so the backing extends beyond the hooked edge and with a needle and thread, tack the cording in place all around the outside of the rug. (Figure 17)

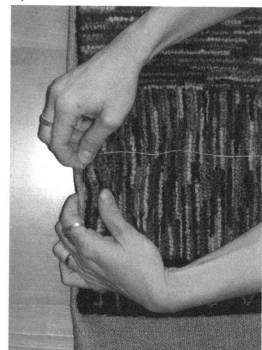

Figure 17

When you come to the corner, wrap the extra linen around the cord, taking care to shape the corner so it looks square from the top. (Figure 18)

Figure 18

On the back, fold the hem down the middle of the corner (Figure 19). Fold the backing down one side of the corner and pin this part down. (Figure 20) Do the same for the other side of the corner hem, so that the two folds meet diagonally. (Figure 21) Don't worry about pinning down the whole hem at this point--let's do the binding first.

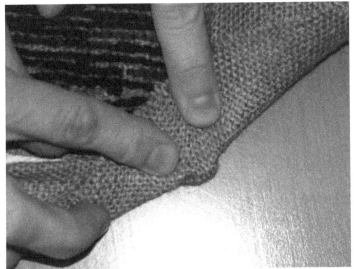

Figure 19

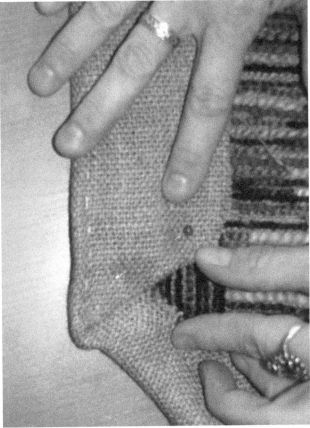

Figure 20

Figure 21

Using a tapestry needle and some matching yarn, you can now bind the edge. First bring your needle up from the back to the front, and leave a small amount of yarn in the back. (Figure 22) Now bring your needle again up from the back to the front, holding the yarn end in your left hand. Keep whip-stitching in this way, sewing over the tail in the back. (Figure 23)

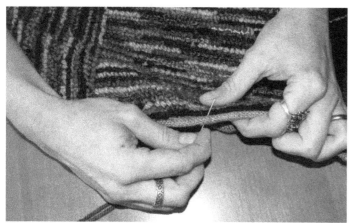
Figure 22

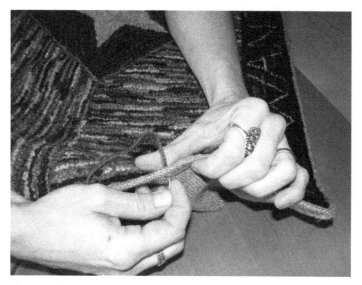
Figure 23

Once you've established your whip stitching, you need to turn the yarn around, so that your final end will come on the back side of the rug. Push your needle into the front of the rug, and bring it out the back. (Figure 24)

Figure 24

Keep stitching until you run out of yarn, leaving a tail sticking out of the back. Thread the needle again, and start from back to front first, sewing over both tails this time. Then turn the yarn around so all the tails end up in the back. Carefully stitch around the corner so all of the linen is covered by yarn. (Figure 25)

Figure 25

When you have whip-stitched all around the edge (you clever thing) push your needle under the stitching in back, so you have your final tail underneath the stitching. Cut the tail so the end disappears in the back. (Figure 26)

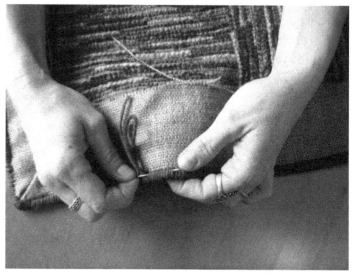
Figure 26

Fold your linen edges under for your hem, and pin in place. With regular needle and thread, hem the rug, making sure you are taking deep stitches, connecting to the backing, not to just a bit of yarn. The goal is not to make dainty, invisible stitches. If you ever have to repair this rug (or if your granddaughter has to repair it!), you will appreciate it if the stitches are easy to find, and you don't have to go digging around looking for them. You should also stitch up the diagonal folds in the corners. (Figure 27)

Press your hem on the back side of the rug with a steam iron.

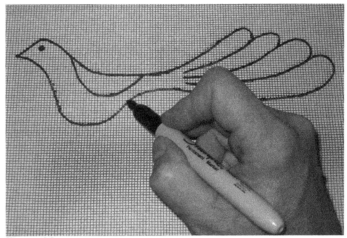

Figure 28

Figure 27

GETTING YOUR DESIGN ONTO LINEN

Draw your design on paper in pencil. When you are happy with your drawing, go over all of your lines with a permanent marker. Next, lay window screen (you can buy this by the roll from a hardware store) over your paper drawing. Trace over all of your lines, thereby transferring your exact design onto the window screen. (Figure 28) Then lay the window screen over your linen and trace over all of the lines again. (Figure 29) When you remove the window screen from the linen, go over all of the lines once again so they show up clearly. (Figure 30)

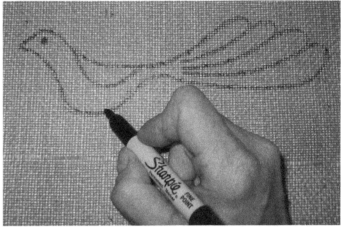

Figure 29

Figure 30

189

CREATING YOUR OWN CABLED YARNS by Dianne Cross

You don't have to be a handspinner to add bulk, texture and mix colours by cabling your yarn.

Cables lend themselves to additional mixing of colour. As a cable consists or four singles, each single can be a different colour or a related colour to give a 'tweedy' look. For subtleness, a variety of shades in one cable yarn works well. I most often use this technique when doing foliage....a variety of shades of greens to browns. Another reason I feel that cables are valuable is that they sit nicely once hooked in the fabric.

Some of my yarn stash

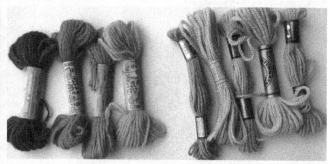
Samples of commercial tapestry yarns

1. Spindle

2. Tying yarn to the spindle hook

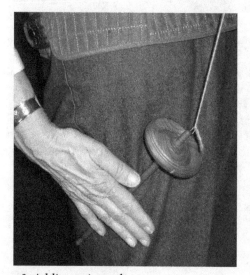
3. Adding twist to the yarn (overplying)

4. Checking for adequate over-twist

5. Folding yarn back on itself (without letting any twist escape, fold the yarn back on itself)

6. Tying yarns of different colours

7. Adding twist to tied yarns

8. Folding over-twisted yarns back (without losing any twist)

Final product, two tapestry yarn colours cabled

Cabling two colours

Two tapestry yarns cabled for shades of colour

An easy way for a non-spinner to make a cable yarn is to break off about a yard of two-ply yarn, tie it to a spindle. (Figure #2) Turn the spindle in the direction so that it increases and tightens the twist in the yarn. (Not so tight that it becomes like wire, figure #3) Then, keeping the yarn under some tension, wrap it around an object at the mid-point of the extended yarn to maintain tension and fold it back in half by bringing the ends together (Figure #5). Hold the ends tightly so that this excess twist does not escape from either end. Now, keeping the tension on the folded yarn, lift it from the mid-point holding object and with the ends together allow it to twist itself into a four strand cable yarn (Figure #8).

For a spinner this can be done, of course, on a spinning wheel in greater lengths.

Handspun wool/mohair blend, cabled

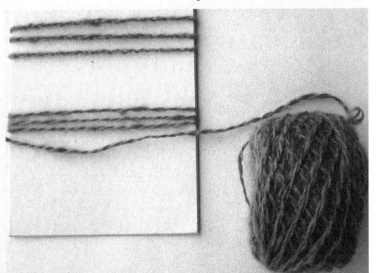